100 DETAILS

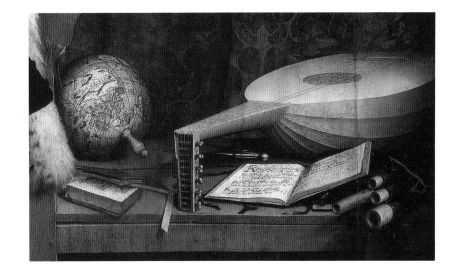

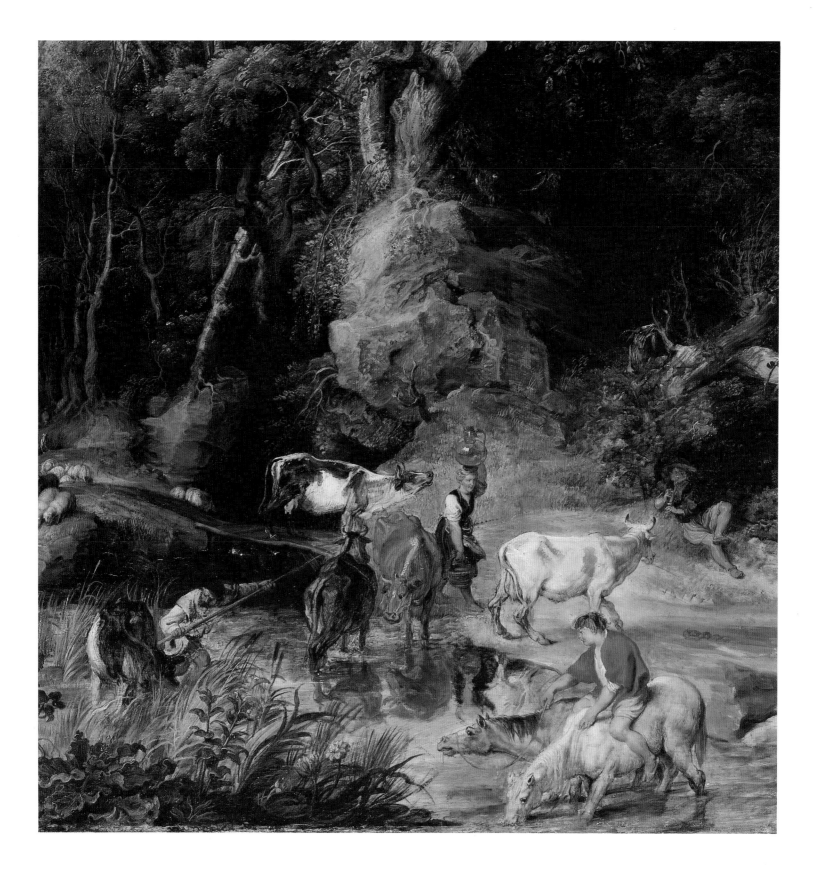

100 DETAILS

FROM PICTURES IN
THE NATIONAL GALLERY

KENNETH CLARK

The National Gallery, London

Harvard University Press
Cambridge, Massachusetts, and London, England
1990

British Library Cataloguing in Publication Data

Clark, Kenneth *1903–1983*
100 details from pictures in the National Gallery, London. –
2nd. ed.
1. Paintings. Catalogues – Indexes
I. Title   II. National Gallery, Great Britain
759

ISBN 0–674–63862–X
ISBN 0–674–63863–8 pbk

Library of Congress Cataloging-in-Publication Data

National Gallery (Great Britain)
[One hundred details from pictures in the National Gallery]
100 details in paintings from the National Gallery, London/with
an introduction and notes by Kenneth Clark.
p.   cm.
Reprint, Originally published: One hundred details from pictures
in the National Gallery, London, 1938.
ISBN 0–674–63862–X (cloth)
0–674–63863–8 (pbk.)
1. Painting—Themes, motives.   2. Painting—Appreciation.
3. National Gallery (Great Britain)   I. Clark, Kenneth, 1903–
II. Title.   III. Title: One hundred details in paintings from the
National Gallery, London.
ND1143.N37   1991
759.94—dc20
90–5358
CIP

Designed by Sara Robin
Printed and bound in Great Britain by
Butler and Tanner Limited, Frome and London

Front cover: Detail from *The Battle of San
Romano* by Uccello.
Back cover: Detail from *Christina of Denmark,
Duchess of Milan* by Holbein.
Half title page: Detail from *The Ambassadors* by Holbein.
Frontispiece: Detail from *The Watering Place* by Rubens.

Editor's Note: Titles, attribution and dates have been altered
as necessary in Kenneth Clark's text in accordance with the
current *National Gallery Illustrated General Catalogue*.

CONTENTS

FOREWORD

The great merit of these photographic details', explained Kenneth Clark in his Preface to the 1938 edition of this book, 'is that they encourage us to look at pictures more attentively.' That would be justification enough for reprinting now. In the fifty intervening years, museums and galleries have become obligatory stops on a much expanded tourist circuit and there has been an unimaginable proliferation of images on television and video: attentive looking is perhaps harder now than ever it was. Perhaps it is even more rewarding as a result.

If this book was the fruit of Clark's eye and intellect, it was no less the fruit of the National Gallery's photographic department. Not the least of Clark's distinctions as Director of the National Gallery was his establishment on a firm footing of a photographic department which was for many years unmatched among the world's great galleries, and which played a central part in the publication and study of the National Gallery's pictures. It continues to do so to this day.

To publish a collection of details in 1938, when the entire National Gallery was poised for evacuation (the pictures were moved out of London at the time of the Munich crisis) was an act of faith. It presupposed a public already familiar with the Collection which would come back to look again, and afresh – a public willing to take pictures seriously and to make them part of their lives, whatever political trials lay ahead.

The venture was novel. Although photographs had become central to any serious art-historical work well before the 1930s, as Clark new at first hand from his visits to the great connoisseur, Bernard Berenson, the use of details was, he explains in his Introduction, still far from common. This must largely have been a result of the practical difficulties of taking good detail shots when few public collections had in-house photographers; yet it is nonetheless surprising, given the incomparable value of such photographs in determining questions of attribution. Indeed modern connoisseurship had tended to concentrate on just those minute particulars – the form of an ear lobe or a finger joint – which photography can so effectively isolate.

Clark makes very considerable attributional use of them here – to defend the *Virgin of the Rocks* as an authentic Leonardo, to promote the *'Manchester Madonna'* as an early Michelangelo (this very convincingly) and to argue, as so often, for the presence of Giorgione's hand on a canvas in the Gallery, in this instance in the background to Titian's *'Noli me Tangere'*.

Clark was keenly alert to the limitations of black-and-white photography for his purposes. Like engraving, it will favour linear art at the expense of the painterly, an injustice intensified by the reduction of focus to a detail, where free brushwork is unlikely to tell to advantage. Perhaps these limitations were welcome, for they directed Clark's choice to the areas of his own predilections – to the Renaissance rather than the

Baroque, to Tuscany rather than Venice, and to questions of form rather than narrative.

There was, however, a further advantage in black-and-white photography: it went a long way to concealing the fact that the National Gallery Collection, like the London atmosphere of the 1930s, was among the dirtiest in the world. In some of his commentaries Clark points out the loss of pleasure caused by discoloured varnish or by clumsy retouchings, uncertain shadows that stand between the spectator and the artist's intentions. But he is also fearful of what might be found if the golden veils of dirt and varnish were ever to be removed. In the years since the war many have been. As they are shown in this edition, Titian's *Bacchus and Ariadne* and Holbein's *Christina of Denmark* are different in critical respects from the paintings Clark discussed. The reader who can compare the earlier edition with this one will decide how much is gain, how much loss.

This is – admittedly and rightly – a personal choice, made by a man of great taste and informed prejudice. Clark chose the pictures he liked, in the hope that we would come to like them too. He insists that there are countless ways of enjoying painting, provided you stop, look and think. He has picked the ones to stop at. The detail makes you look. And his comments, wide in scope and catholic in approach, suggest lines of thought so diverse that it is inconceivable that none will strike a chord with the reader.

These fifty or so captions – they are hardly more – are Clark at his best. They range from a few lines to an entire history of still life between Giotto and Picasso. The easy style, so nearly that of a radio talk, makes no attempt at all to conceal the width of its erudition. World history and world culture are taken at the gallop, and with a smile. Raphael is ticked off for 'sailing close to the wind', and is then at once likened to Racine or Mozart; Matteo di Giovanni is compared to African sculpture; Piero to the drunken Wu-Wei or a Sung ink-painter; and most arrestingly of all, Beccafumi to Sickert. Gerard David's tranquil Richardus de Capella and his well-laundered surplice Clark dispatches, with Thomas Carlyle's blessing, to historical oblivion. And the note that starts with a jaunty reference to the 'cockney vitality' of Hogarth's cat finishes with Paul Bourget's gnomic evocation, in French, of the physique of Walter Pater.

In discussing Plates 10 and 11 Clark, I believe, goes to the heart of our pleasure in paintings. He imagines the inquisitive little girl from Crivelli's *Annunciation* peering round the corner at the Netherlandish townscape in Campin's *Virgin and Child before a Fire-screen*. The pictures themselves have different subjects and different scales; many decades, the Alps and all the Rhine lie between them. The choice of the details, however, by leaving all other considerations on one side, highlights sharply the totality of painting as a fiction entire unto itself, an imagined world inviting exploration, where we can in time feel at home and move about with confidence. Only familiarity with pictures, only regular looking, can give that freedom to roam through an imagined world which is one of the great delights of the spirit and which is perhaps the principal purpose of the National Gallery.

NEIL MacGREGOR
DIRECTOR

INTRODUCTION

This book contains one hundred photographic reproductions of details taken from pictures in the National Gallery. They have been chosen chiefly for their beauty, and since two details must face one another when the book is opened, they have been arranged in such a way as to bring out certain analogies and contrasts. Some of these contrasts are like epigrammatic summaries of the history of art, in particular those at the beginning of the book, which show the differences between Northern and Mediterranean painting. But the majority of openings have been arranged because the details have something in common, either of movement and design or of subject and mood. Violent contrasts have been avoided lest they should destroy the beauty of the individual pictures; for the platitude that great works of art of any epoch always go well together is untrue. Great pictures grumble at each other, insult or even annihilate each other as often as great men.

As with any form of anthology, the choice must ultimately reflect the taste of the chooser, and this may be one reason why so many details are taken from Italian painting of the fifteenth and sixteenth centuries. But there is another reason, that pictures in a style based on firm delineation, a style requiring equal finish in all the parts, yield far better details than pictures in what may be called an impressionist style, where the degree of finish grows less as the eye moves away from the focal point.

Although almost all the details are beautiful in themselves, a few are chosen for historical or iconographical reasons, as for example Bassano's malicious portrait of the aged Titian (Plate 20); and a few others were included because they were so unexpected. Even those who know the Gallery well may not have noticed the quarrel between a bear and a lion in Filippino's *Virgin and Child* (Plate 65). The landscape in Plate 43 comes from one of the most familiar of all pictures, yet some people may fail to recognise it at the first glance. And how many will recall the source of Plate 10 or, for that matter, of Plate 54?

Our failure to recognise some of these details may provide an amusing game; it also has an important meaning. It means that we do not look at pictures carefully. There was much to be said for the old naïve method by which people read a picture like a book. We, in our anxiety to avoid a literary approach, are often content with a quick synthetic impression. It may be true that a work of art can be recognised in the first second, but this does not exhaust its potentialities. The great value of these photographic details is that they encourage us to look at pictures more attentively, and show us some of the rewards of patient scrutiny. They are, in fact, an aid to appreciation more valuable, because more concrete, than the numerous books on how to look at pictures. They fulfil one of the first functions of criticism by presenting familiar material from a fresh point of view. This is particularly true of large pictures when, for physical reasons alone, it is difficult to give equal attention to all the parts. Take Matteo di Giovanni's *Assumption of the Virgin*. We have all seen her head, but from a distance of about twelve feet, and the reproduction on Plate 36 reveals a firmness and simplicity of drawing which the most attentive gaze could not perceive from below. The angels which surround her are too numerous for us easily to appreciate their individual graces; in detail they provide some of the most beautiful pictures in the book (Plate 89). Another example is the distant landscape high up in the Pollaiuolo brothers' huge *Martyrdom of Saint Sebastian*, which turns out to be worthy of a place opposite Rubens's *Autumn Landscape* (Plate 26).

Although the beauty of such details seems obvious to us, they had been taken for scientific purposes for many years before anyone thought of reproducing them for their own sakes; and I believe it was the Japanese critic Yukio Yashiro who first used them as aids to appreciation in his book on Botticelli. From a scientific point of view full-size photographs are often very misleading. We are so accustomed to making allowances for reduction of scale, that photographs the size of the original make anything but the most polished handling look rough. As a result, a painter such as Bronzino is flattered, whereas the details from Piero della Francesca's *Nativity* are so disappointing that none has been included. [In the 1938 edition the details were reproduced in black and white, and many were almost the actual size of the original.]

I have written a note to almost every plate or pair of plates. Some of these notes contain scraps of information or criticism which may interest students, but as a whole they are intended for the general reader. They represent the kind of conversation which two people fond of painting might have while going round the National Gallery. One good result of this informal method is that every note shows a different approach, for nothing is more fatal to criticism than the fallacy of one cause. Just as a great river does not flow from a single source, but is made up of innumerable tributaries great and small, so the total impression of a work of art is built up of a hundred different sensations, analogies, memories, thoughts – some obvious, many recondite, a few analysable, most beyond analysis. Faithfully to record, in front of concrete examples, whatever impressions the moment admits, suits the informal arrangement of the book as a whole, and allows me to set down certain ideas which might not otherwise find expression and which may start trains of thought in the reader's mind.

KENNETH CLARK
1938

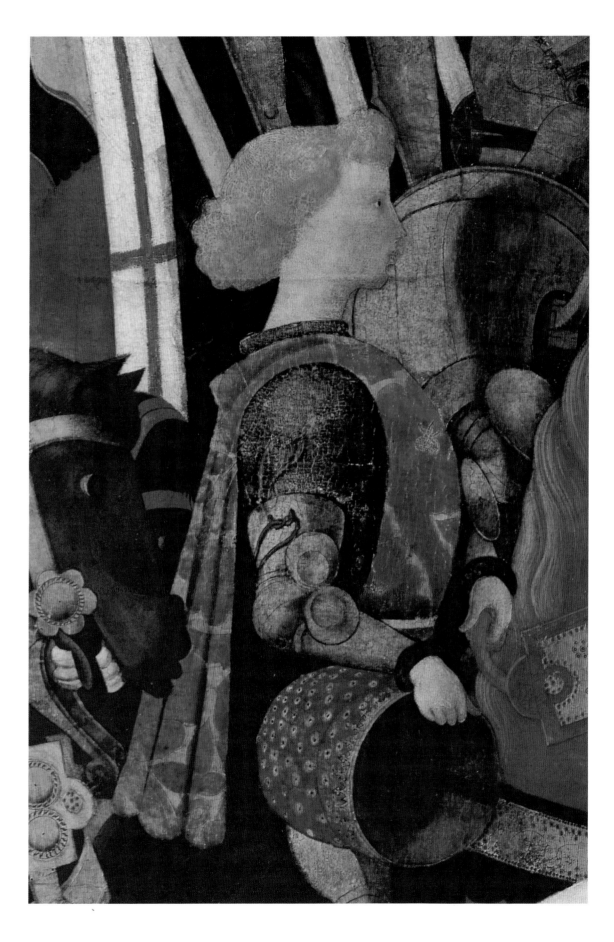

Nicholas of Tolentino's Page from THE BATTLE OF SAN ROMANO *by Uccello, painted in the 1450s.*

This beautiful head, the embodiment of youthful chivalry, should dispose of the idea that *The Battle of San Romano* is no more than a glorified nursery picture. It is not only one of the finest pieces of colour and design in the Gallery but shows that Uccello was capable of creating a world more vital than the classical painting of the next century and no less authentically ideal.

Giovanni Arnolfini from the
ARNOLFINI MARRIAGE
by van Eyck, painted in 1434.

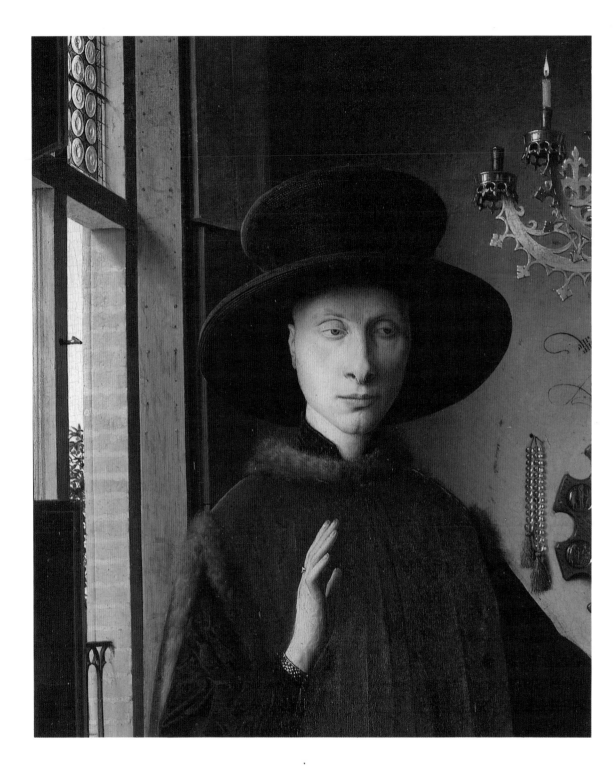

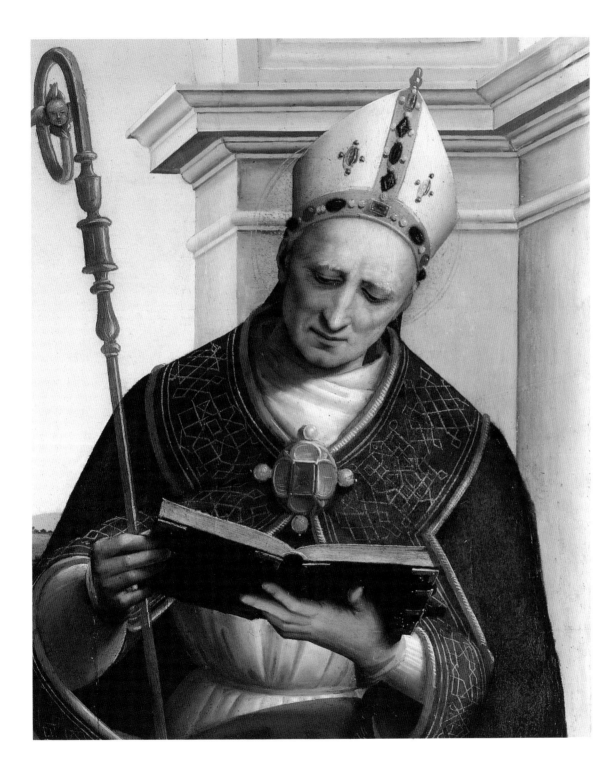

Saint Nicholas of Bari from
THE ANSIDEI MADONNA
by Raphael, painted in 1505.

The book contains several contrasts between North and South, between the Gothic naturalism of Flemish painting and the scientific humanism of Italian; but none more complete and essential than this. In the van Eyck the forms are thin and asymmetrical – the face under its disproportionate hat, the hand, the flame of the candle. In the Raphael they are large and geometrical. They obey the laws which man's intelligence has imposed on durable materials, in architecture or machinery. The *'Arnolfini Marriage'* is like a flower, developing its tissue according to the laws of natural growth. This dwelling on a substance for its own sake is extended to inorganic objects like the brass candlestick, whereas Saint Nicholas's crozier is merely a generalised shape in the balance of the composition. I find that these details are complementary to one another. The van Eyck brings out the wonderful plastic sequences of the Raphael, but has a delicacy of perception both physical and spiritual, which Raphael has excluded.

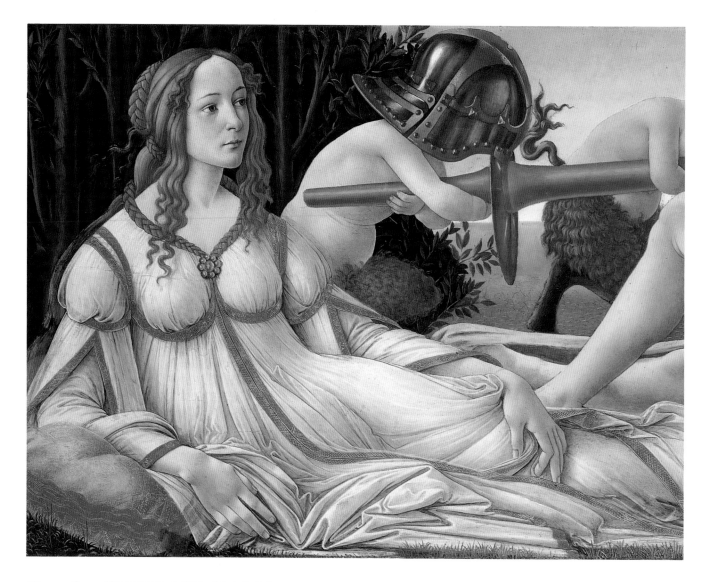

Venus from VENUS AND MARS *by Botticelli, painted about 1480.*

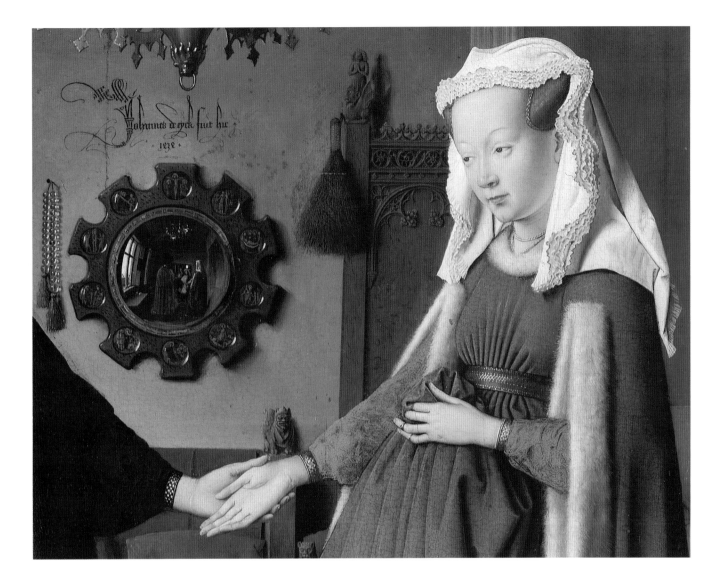

Giovanna Cenami from the ARNOLFINI
MARRIAGE *by van Eyck, painted in 1434.*

The confrontation of two such profoundly different
pictures borders on sacrilege, but may, I hope, be
forgiven for the clear and concentrated way in which it
expresses two opposing pictorial ideals. Moreover, it
supplements the comparison of Flemish and Italian
painting attempted in the notes to Plates 2 and 3, 6 and 7,
the points at issue being rather different. Should a painter
create a new world of beauty out of his imagination? Or
should he content himself with painting what he sees
and trust that beauty will grow out of the actual seeing
and rendering? These details show that he can do either,
if in each case his vision is sufficiently coherent. It is
tempting to say that the Botticelli is poetry, the van Eyck
prose, but like most analogies between the arts it is
untrue, for a painter's joy in the perception of light
passing over a white cloth can only be called poetical.

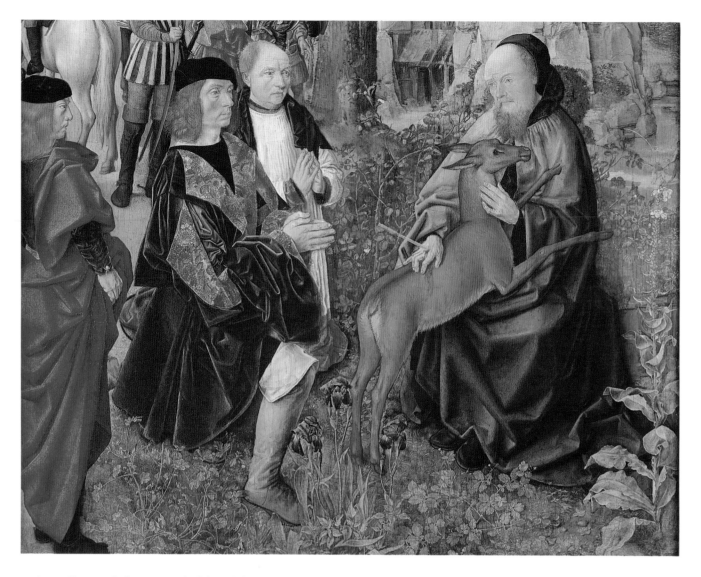

Saint Giles and the wounded hind from
SAINT GILES AND THE HIND *by the*
Master of Saint Giles, painted about 1500.

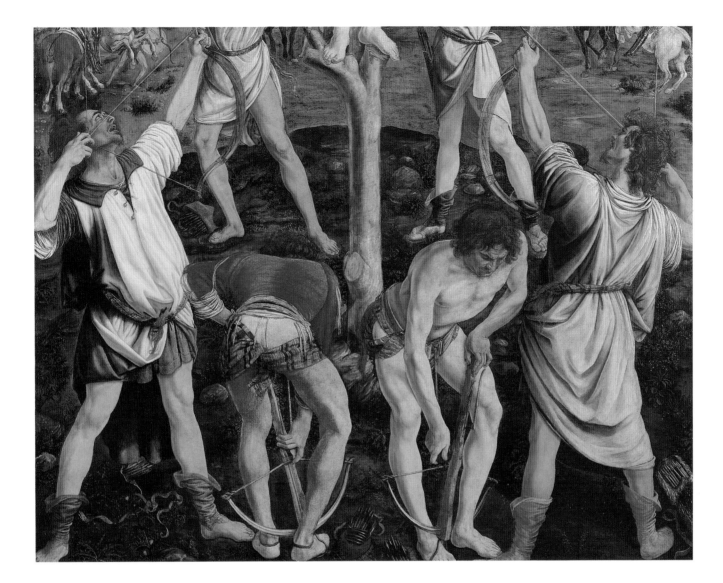

A group of archers from **THE MARTYRDOM OF SAINT SEBASTIAN,** *by Antonio and Piero del Pollaiuolo, painted about 1475.*

The contrast between North and South, analysed in the notes to Plates 2 and 3, 4 and 5, can here be brought out by a mere description of the subjects. Saint Giles is protecting a deer, wounded by an arrow which has pierced the saint's own hand. The huntsman, dressed in a voluminous cloak of velvet and brocade, kneels in expiation, surrounded by clusters of wild flowers – iris, hollyhock, wild strawberry, wood spurge, briar rose – all most lovingly drawn. The Pollaiuolo brothers disclose a very different world. No fuss about flowers, no pother about a wounded animal. Six magnificent ruffians are discharging their arrows at the naked, defenceless body of a young man. From the ethical point of view perhaps the Northern picture is preferable, but the Pollaiuolo

brothers were not concerned with ethics. They were concerned with the science of picture-making in which, to the Florentine mind, the most important part was the rendering of movement and the most notable subject *un bel corpo ignudo*. Their subject is merely a pretext for a play of muscle; and in consequence we feel less sympathy for the tortured saint than for the wounded deer. On the contrary our sympathy is with the archers, whose magnificent vigour is invigorating to us. The two men in the foreground bending over their crossbows are one of the best examples in art of those ideated sensations which Bernard Berenson made the basis of his essay on Florentine painting (*The Florentine Painters of the Renaissance*, 1896).

7

Saint Catherine and the donor, Richardus de Capella, from THE VIRGIN AND CHILD WITH SAINTS AND DONOR *by Gerard David, painted between 1500 and 1511.*

David is the interpreter of a bland, unruffled piety which the merchants of the Netherlands demanded of their painters, in reaction, perhaps, against the bleeding hearts, flagellated Christs and other violent emblems of popular religion which were common throughout the fifteenth century. 'Above all, no enthusiasm': it is the forced tranquillity which preludes a revolution. In less than twenty years Luther will have appeared on the scene and Richardus de Capella, with his well-ironed surplice over a fur coat, will have vanished, as Carlyle would say, into oblivion. Unfortunately for the theorists, however, this complacent bourgeoisie had inspired a great school of painting, while the succeeding period produced, with rolling of eyes and gnashing of teeth, fewer good works of art than any century since the Dark Ages.

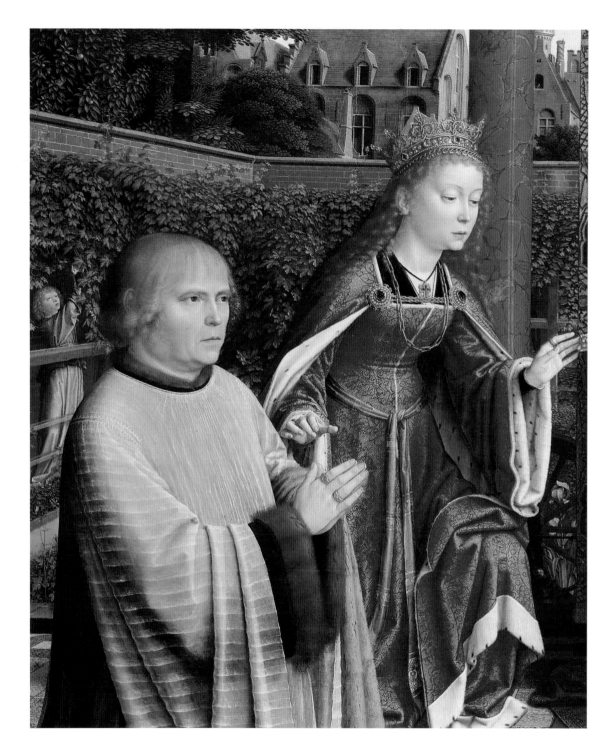

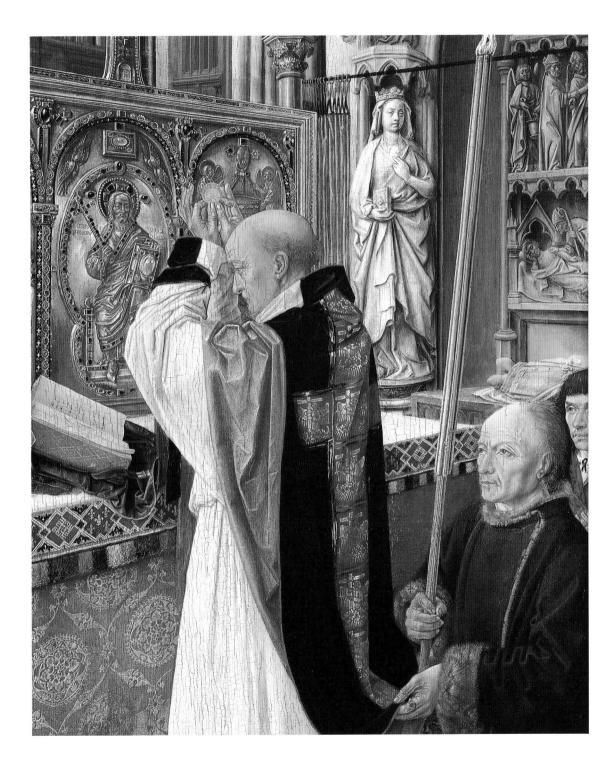

From THE MASS OF
SAINT GILES *by the
Master of Saint Giles,
painted about 1500.*

Apart from its beauty this picture is
a most important archaeological
document, for it contains represen-
tations of the lost treasures of the
Abbey of St Denis, near Paris. These
are described in old inventories, and
we can see how accurately the
painter has imitated the originals,
only reducing their scale in relation
to his figures. This detail shows the
golden retable which had been
presented to the Abbey by Charles
the Bald in the ninth century, and
was destroyed in the French
Revolution.

A child from
THE ANNUNCIATION
by Crivelli, painted in 1486.

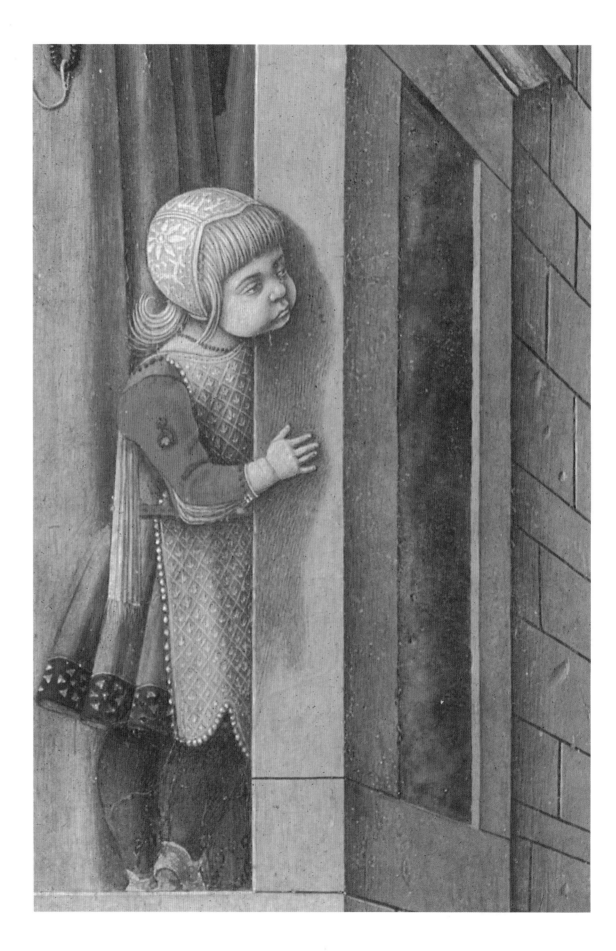

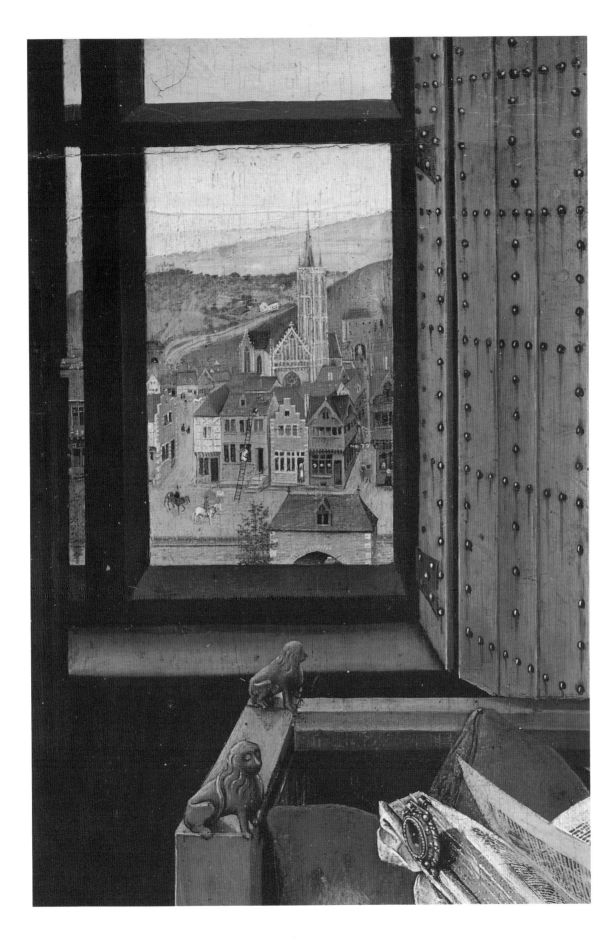

A view through a window from THE VIRGIN AND CHILD BEFORE A FIRE- SCREEN *by Campin, painted before 1430.*

The small child from Crivelli's *Annunciation* looks round the corner of a balcony and sees through 'Campin's' window a beautiful toy town, brighter and more real than anything she could have found in Italian painting of the time.

A faun from
A MYTHOLOGICAL
SUBJECT *by Piero di Cosimo,*
painted about 1500.

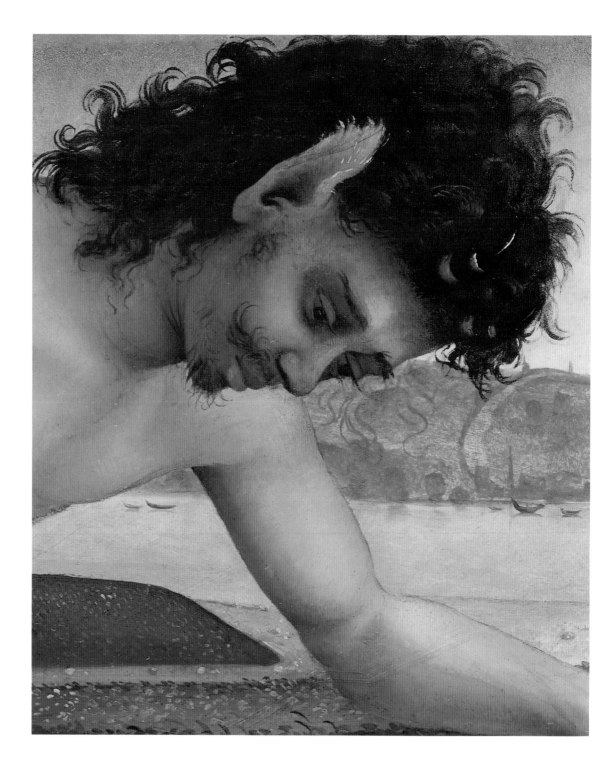

[1] The Chatsworth drawing is not of a
faun, but of a malformed boy; taken
with the inscription, possibly in
Carracci's own hand, the effect is not
tender, nor subtle, nor sentimental,
but heart-rending.

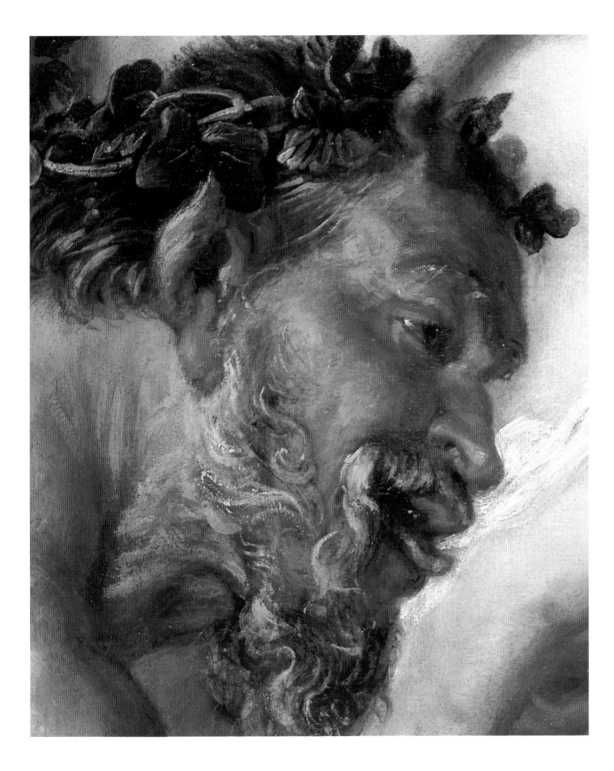

After long banishment those hairy devils of the Middle Ages, the satyrs, returned to a popularity greater than they had known in antiquity, for in the Renaissance they were no longer part of a living superstition, and so no longer alarming. Archaeology tamed but did not convert them. They remained symbols of sensuality unobstructed by conscience, and it is not surprising to find them, in the portable form of bronzes by Riccio and his school, among the minor household gods of the sixteenth century. But they even survived the Counter Reformation, appearing in force round Ammanati's fountain in the Piazza della Signoria, Florence; and they populated the imaginative painting of the Seicento, on Carracci's ceiling (Palazzo Farnese, Rome), in Poussin's Bacchanals and in the work of Rubens, who gives them their full, lusty force, and something of the country coarseness which was part of their original character. The distinction between satyrs and fauns, already lost in Roman literature, is hardly ever observed. Nearly all the satyrs have goats' feet, and the fauns have lost their divinity. But Piero di Cosimo, in his devoted reading of antique poetry, has discovered the original faun, the shy, half-human creature for which he had an especial tenderness. It was a conception too subtle and sentimental for the sixteenth century as a whole, but there is a Carracci drawing of a faun at Chatsworth which bears the inscription *non so se dio m'ajuta* (I do not know if God is helping me), and this is close enough to the spirit of Piero di Cosimo.[1]

A scoffer from CHRIST MOCKED *by Hieronymus Bosch, painted about 1500.*

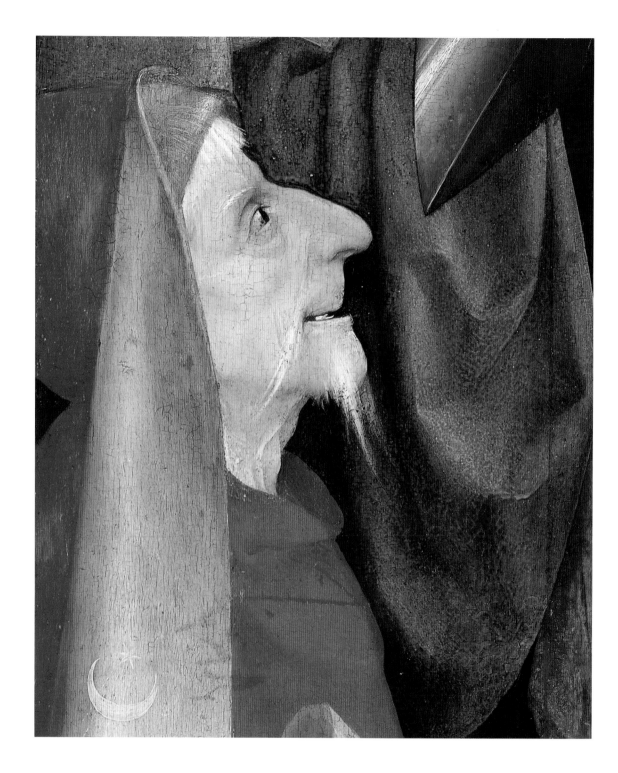

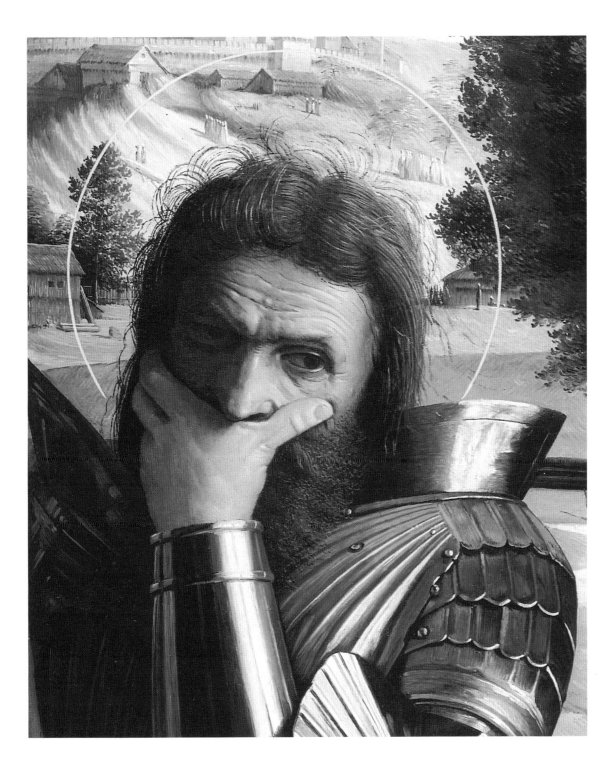

Saint Demetrius from
**SAINTS SEBASTIAN,
ROCH AND DEMETRIUS**
*by L'Ortolano, painted
before 1516.*

The connection between Hieronymus Bosch and that dreary Ferrarese, L'Ortolano, is unexpected, yet these heads go well enough together because both have an element of expressionism, a slight over-emphasis rare in Italian art. The detail of Bosch's Shakespearean clown shows the sensibility of touch which distinguishes his work from that of his imitators, past and present. The head of Saint Demetrius must be far the most striking thing L'Ortolano ever did, and results from a judicious mixture of Roman and Venetian influences. The motif of the hand covering mouth and beard seems to have been invented by Leonardo in his sketches for the Uffizi *Adoration of the Magi* and thence borrowed by Raphael for the figure of Saint Paul in his *Saint Cecilia* (Pinacoteca, Bologna). The eclectic L'Ortolano must have seen Raphael's altarpiece in the neighbouring town of Bologna and in this picture he has turned the figure round to face the spectator; and he has added a romantic spirit deriving from Giorgione.

15

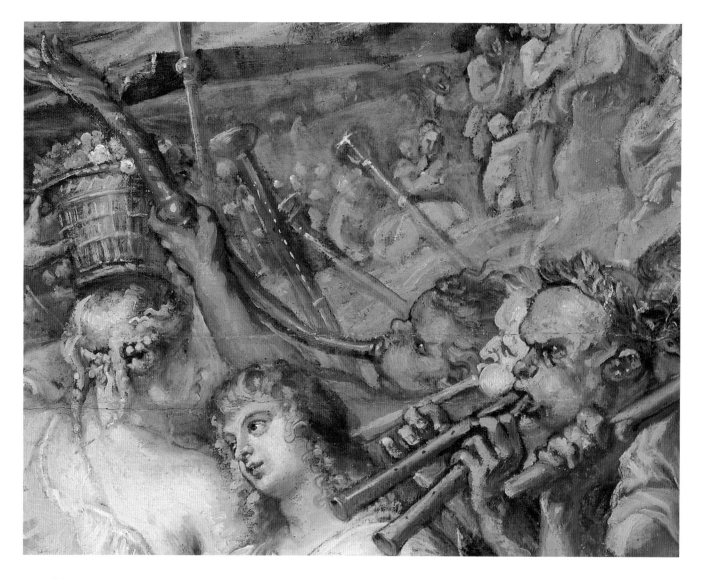

Musicians from A ROMAN TRIUMPH *by Rubens, painted about 1630.*

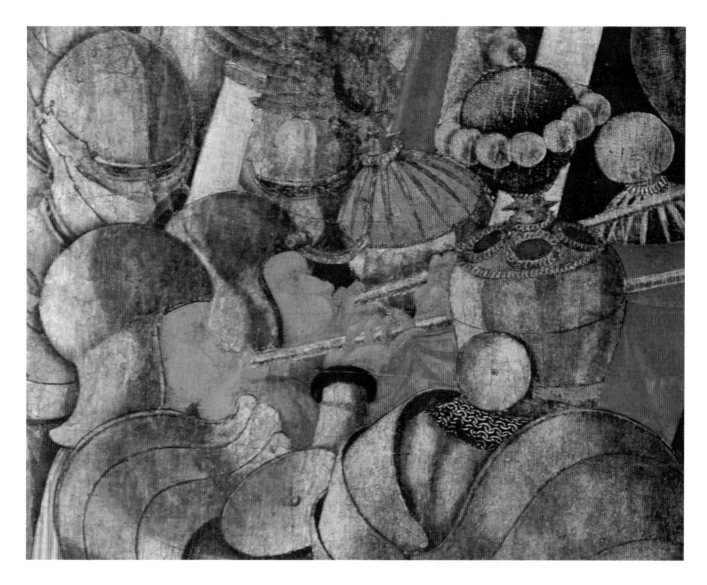

Trumpeters from THE BATTLE OF SAN ROMANO *by Uccello, painted in the 1450s.*

The contrast in handling is too obvious for exposition, and is made more striking by the fact that Rubens is actually following, with considerable freedom, a Renaissance design.

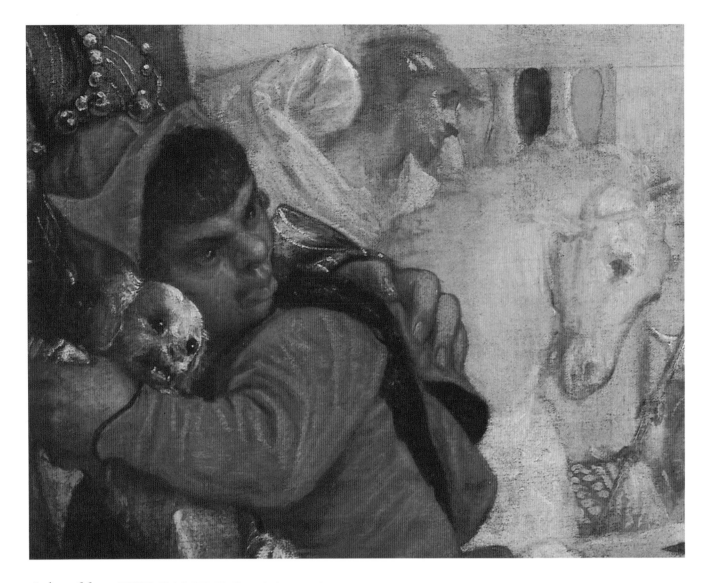

A dwarf from THE FAMILY OF DARIUS
BEFORE ALEXANDER *by Veronese,*
painted in the 1570s.

Paolo Veronese must have been one of the first great painters to introduce figures into his pictures purely for their decorative or picturesque value, without regard to dramatic significance. In this he was the reverse of his great contemporary, Tintoretto, to whom the drama of the composition as a whole was all-important. As Veronese said himself, 'If there is any space left over in a picture I adorn it with figures according to my invention.' So there was a critical, as well as a religious meaning in the condemnation pronounced on him by the Inquisition in 1573 for putting 'buffoons, drunkards, Germans and similar scurrilities' into his great picture of the *Feast in the House of Levi* (Accademia, Venice). Paolo Veronese might have replied with the scholastic definition of art *quod visum placet*, for there was never a greater master of what pleases the eye. Actually he tried to defend himself by referring to the naked figures in Michelangelo's *Last Judgement* in the Sistine Chapel, and received a well-directed snub, for, as the Inquisitor said, in those figures there is nothing which is not spiritual – *in quelle figure non vi è cosa se non de spirito.*

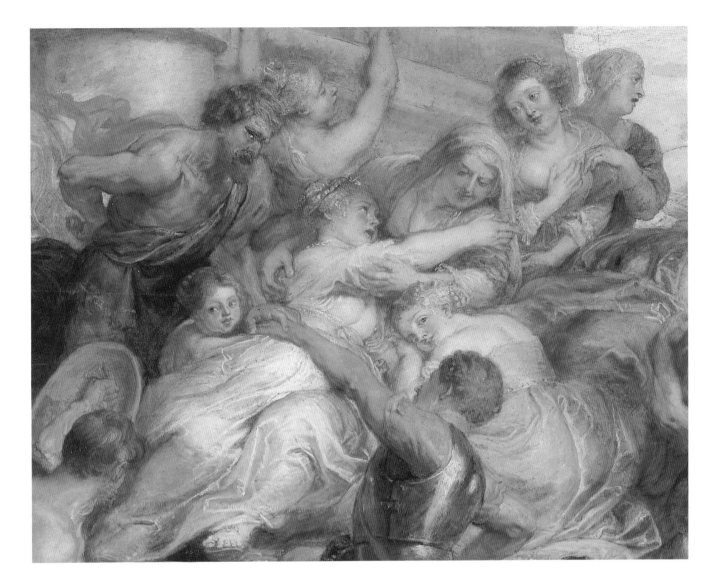

From THE RAPE OF THE SABINE
WOMEN *by Rubens, painted about 1635–40.*

Rubens's love of life is so great that we do not stop to
analyse his mastery of the technique of painting. In this
composition the marvellous skill with which he has built
up a series of rhythmic sequences – curves enclosed in
contrasted diagonals, like fish in a net – is forgotten in
our general sense of exhilaration. The whole group has
the sparkle and buoyancy of the waves. To our eyes there
is something rather charming in the lack of reluctance
shown by most of the victims, and the way in which the
older ladies urge any who are nervous to take the matter
in the right spirit. But a hundred years ago the author of a
guide to the Gallery, criticising Hazlitt's famous
description of the picture as 'plump, florid viragos
struggling with bearded ruffians', said: 'everyone knows
that most women when thus rudely and suddenly
assailed are florid with indignation.'

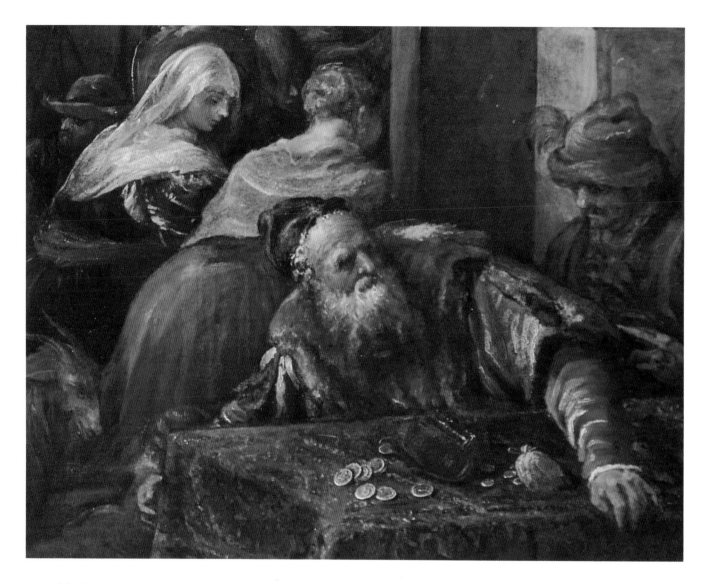

An elderly money changer from
THE PURIFICATION OF THE TEMPLE
by Jacopo Bassano, painted in the 1580s.

The old man is a portrait of Titian, notorious among his
colleagues for his love of money. Bassano has even
caricatured one of Titian's own self portraits, now in the
Gemäldegalerie, Berlin, adapting the pose to one who is
trying to shield his possessions.

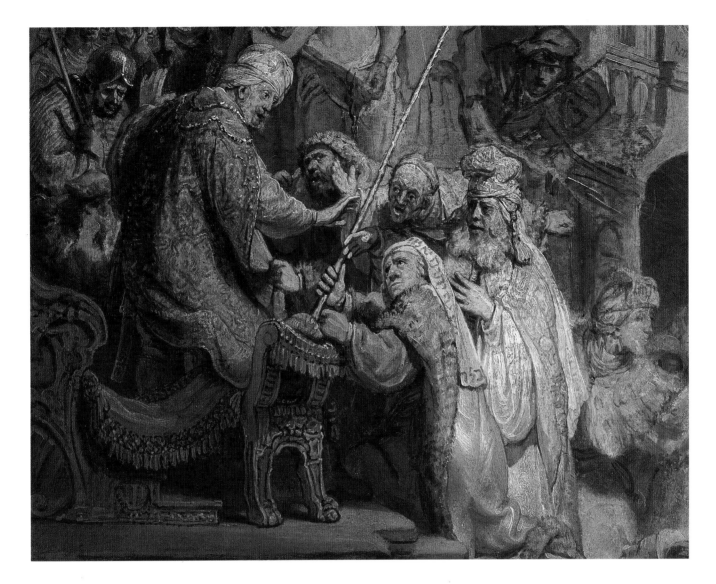

Pilate and the Jews from ECCE HOMO *by Rembrandt, painted in 1634.*

Early Rembrandts are, on the whole, the ugliest pictures ever produced by a supremely great artist. Yet they show an uncompromising devotion to the truth which is most impressive. Rembrandt would not accept the second-hand imagery by which his contemporaries were content to render religious and historical subjects; he would not allow himself the technical tricks by which they evaded difficulties of drawing. He would not deviate from the truth of his imagination. This stubborn integrity, so closely resembling that of the young Cézanne, led to crudities which are sometimes almost insupportable; but even the worst of them have great dramatic force. In this detail, after the first shock has worn off, we become aware of the psychological skill with which the various types of pomposity, bestiality and hysteria are contrasted: Pilate, timid, commonplace, watery-eyed, is like the chairman of an unsuccessful company assailed by angry shareholders. And all these dramatic inventions are set down with an intensity which, for the moment, makes the conventions of more polite painting seem empty and insincere.

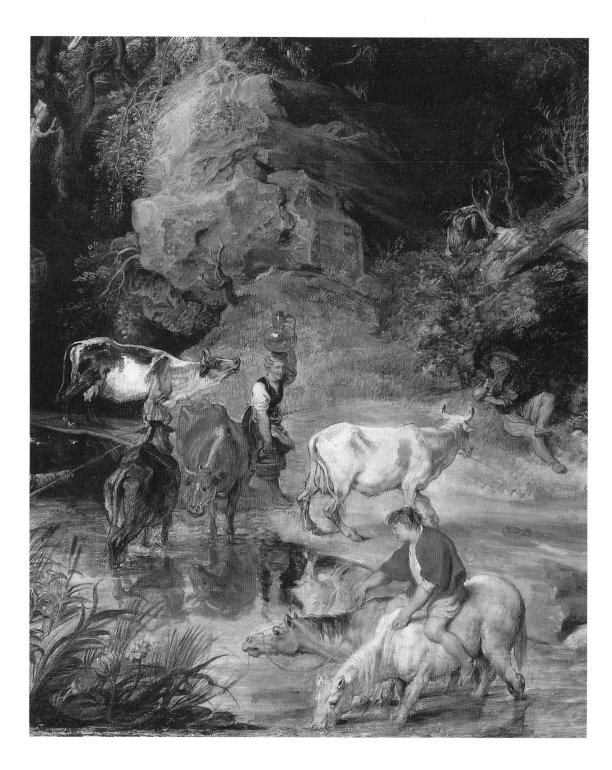

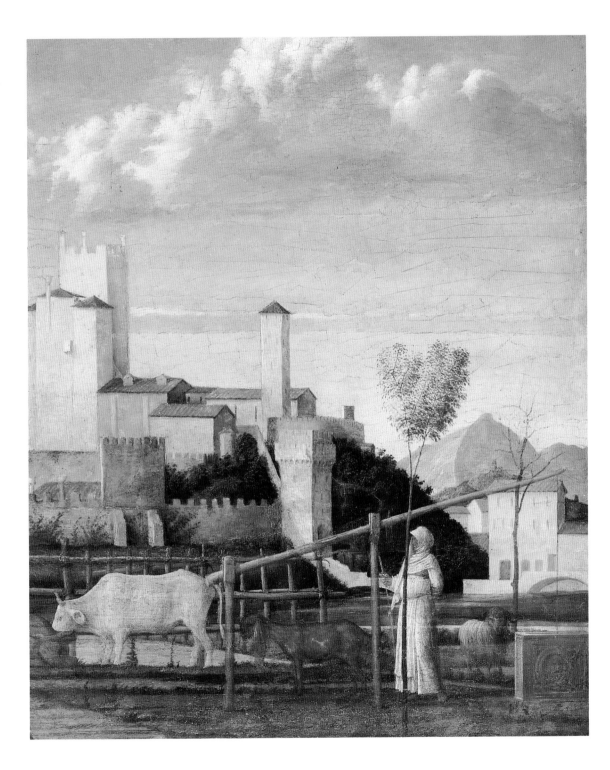

From THE MADONNA OF THE MEADOW *by Giovanni Bellini, painted about 1500.*

These details provide the fullest measure of contrast in the book, and show that extraordinary change in the sense of space which characterises the transition from Renaissance to Baroque. Bellini thinks of space as something static, orderly and limited. His walls and palings, even his cows and goats, are parallel with the picture plane. For the most part they are horizontal, and these horizontals are set off by a series of beautifully spaced verticals, towers, posts, trees and the white-robed shepherd. Each interval is calculated with a sense of finality, as if nature had crystallised at some moment of perfection, and would never again be disturbed. We are reminded of Seurat. Turn to Rubens and space has become dynamic. Everything is in movement – not random movement, but that surging, twisting rhythm we call Baroque. Cows and horses are grouped to combine with the landscape in a great S, and this rhythm is repeated in every detail of roots and rocks. Only the greatest Baroque architects, Bernini and Borromini, had this power of keeping both masses and details moving to the same tune.

From **PORTRAIT OF A BOY** *by a painter of the Florentine School, mid-1540s.*

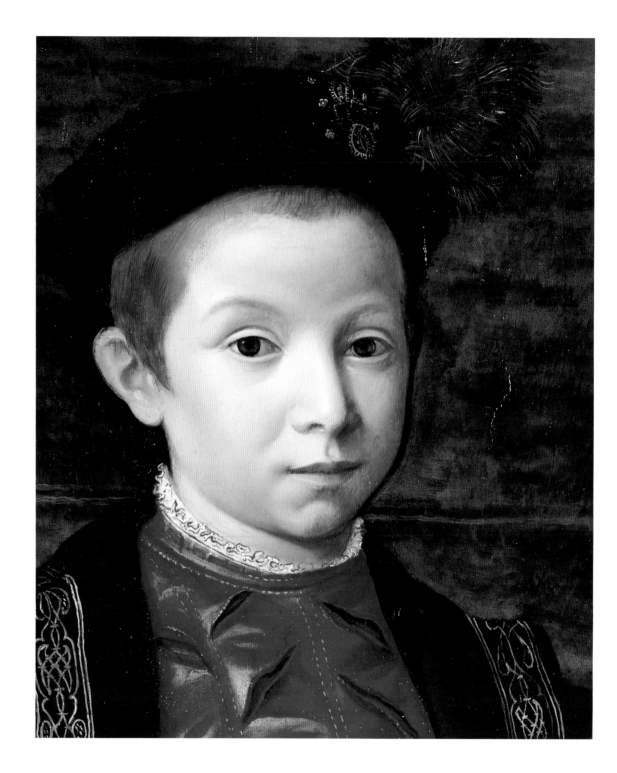

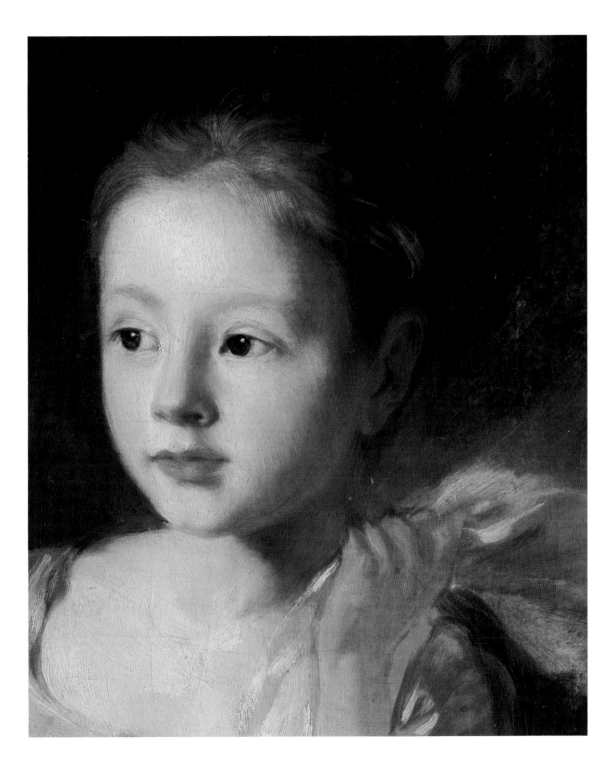

Mary Gainsborough from THE PAINTER'S DAUGHTERS CHASING A BUTTERFLY *by Gainsborough, painted before 1759.*

There is a superficial likeness between the children, and both painters have enjoyed the delicate contours of their youthful faces. But these resemblances only make more clear a fundamental difference of style. The Italian delineates where Gainsborough suggests. Not to be stiff, this linear style must be done with great mastery, and the eyes of the young boy show no real understanding of structure. Mary Gainsborough's eyes are far better drawn. Yet the Florentine artist preserves from a great tradition a more complete sense of plastic unity. He is working within a convention where even a duffer may achieve something if the subject is favourable and he will only keep to the rules.

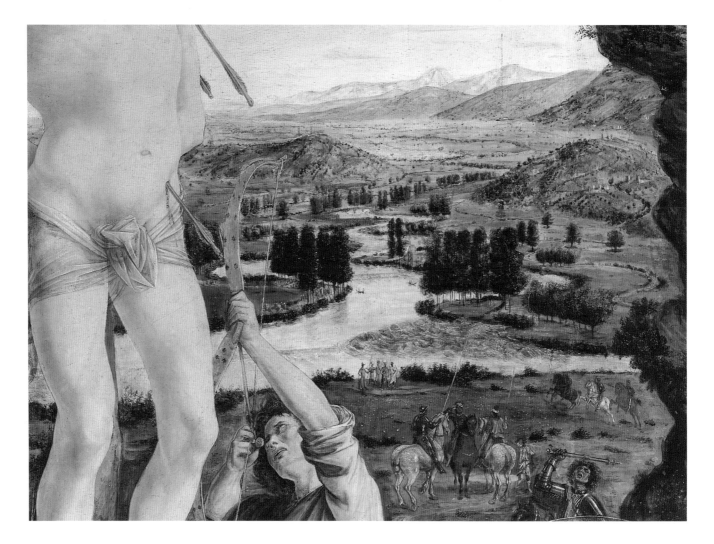

The Val d'Arno from THE MARTYRDOM
OF SAINT SEBASTIAN, *by Antonio
and Piero del Pollaiuolo, painted about 1475.*

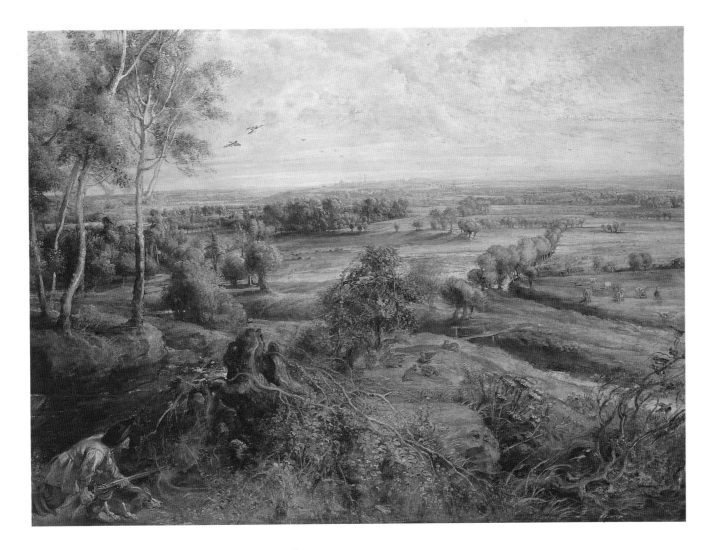

From AN AUTUMN LANDSCAPE *by Rubens, painted in 1636.*

The background of Rubens's *Autumn Landscape* must be one of the greatest of all paintings of a distant landscape; yet the Pollaiuolos' *Val d' Arno*, a small part of a great figure-piece, withstands the comparison, and we are led to ask why, when landscape had been brought to this pitch of perfection by 1475, it had to wait over a hundred years before being recognised as an independent branch of painting. There is no easy answer. Fifteenth-century painters like the Pollaiuolos, Bellini and Perugino loved the subject and painted it with mastery. Leonardo added science to observation in a way not attempted again until Turner. In part the answer must lie with the Renaissance men of letters who had already evolved the classic theory of aesthetics by which a picture was not serious unless the subject was drawn from sacred or heroic literature. But this theory was even more powerful in the seventeenth century, the first great age of landscape, when Claude and Poussin had to call their pictures by fancy titles in order to give the critics something to write about. We cannot explain this period of landscape by any literary parallel such as can be made to cover the revival of landscape painting in the early nineteenth century. Perhaps the only true explanation is the superficial one: Mannerism and eclecticism had so exhausted the figurative arts that without the learning of Poussin and the mature endowment of Rubens no further advance in that direction was possible and painters turned to a branch of the art which still allowed some possibility of unforced expression.

These details show an interesting technical point: the difficulty all early landscape painters experienced in passing from the foreground to the background. The Pollaiuolo brothers and other early Italian painters evaded this difficulty by placing the scene of action on a plateau so that the middle distance was cut out. Rubens has covered up his failure by brilliance of handling, but if we look carefully we see that the space between the over-life-size partridges and the minute footbridge is not realised at all. Claude usually dealt with the problem by a series of *coulisses*. The first painter to whom the middle distance seems to have had no difficulties was Rembrandt, who in his drawings leads the eye smoothly from foreground to background with a few strokes of the pen.

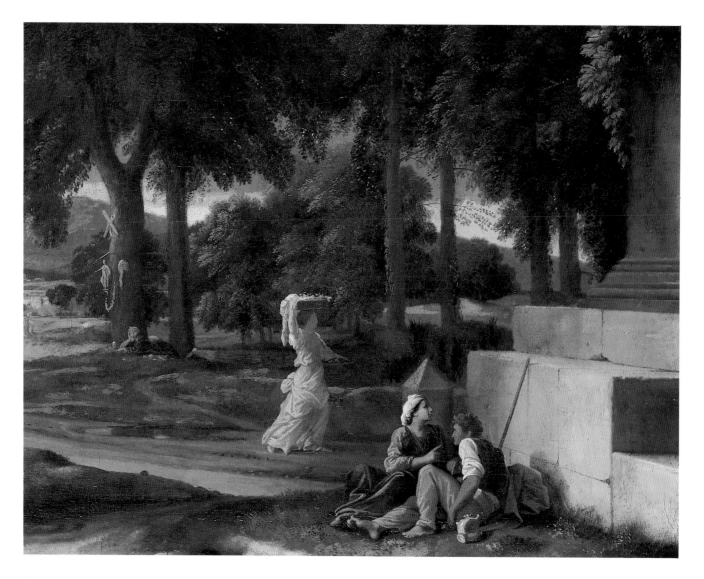

From LANDSCAPE WITH FIGURES,
attributed to Poussin, painted in the late 1640s.

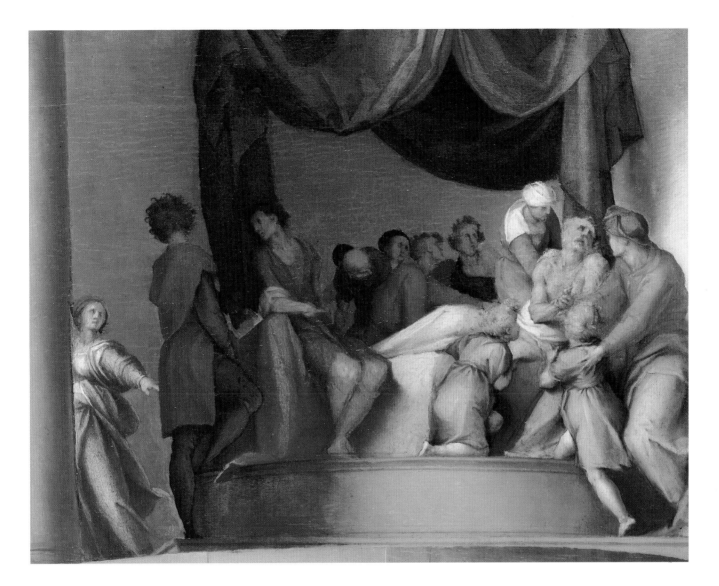

The death of Jacob from JOSEPH WITH JACOB IN EGYPT *by Pontormo, painted about 1515.*

Two examples of details forming complete compositions in themselves. The Pontormo group must generally pass unnoticed in that weird agglomeration of incidents of which it forms a relatively unimportant part. It is strange that Poussin and Pontormo, who represent to the full two opposed systems of design, classicism and Mannerism, should unite so harmoniously; and no doubt the harmony is partly accidental, due to the looped drapery of the Pontormo echoing the rhythm of Poussin's branches, and the pointing woman, who is a principal figure in both scenes. Closer analysis shows how Pontormo has avoided the simple uprights and measured intervals of Poussin, and has achieved a characteristic nervousness, bordering on hysteria. Actually he became an incurable neurasthenic, and kept a diary in which he recorded how many ounces of food he ate at every meal.

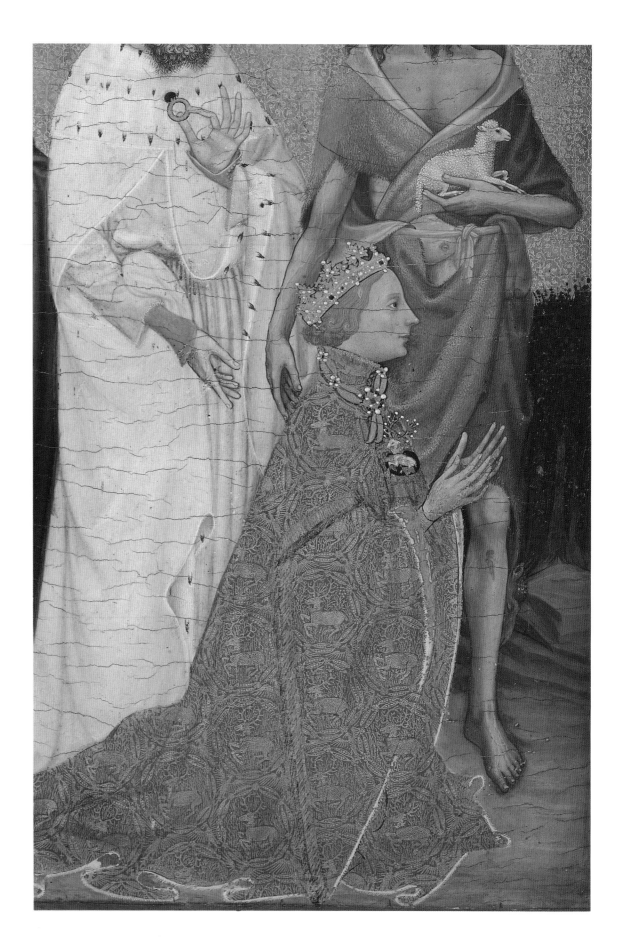

King Richard II from
THE WILTON DIPTYCH
probably by a French painter
working in England about 1395.

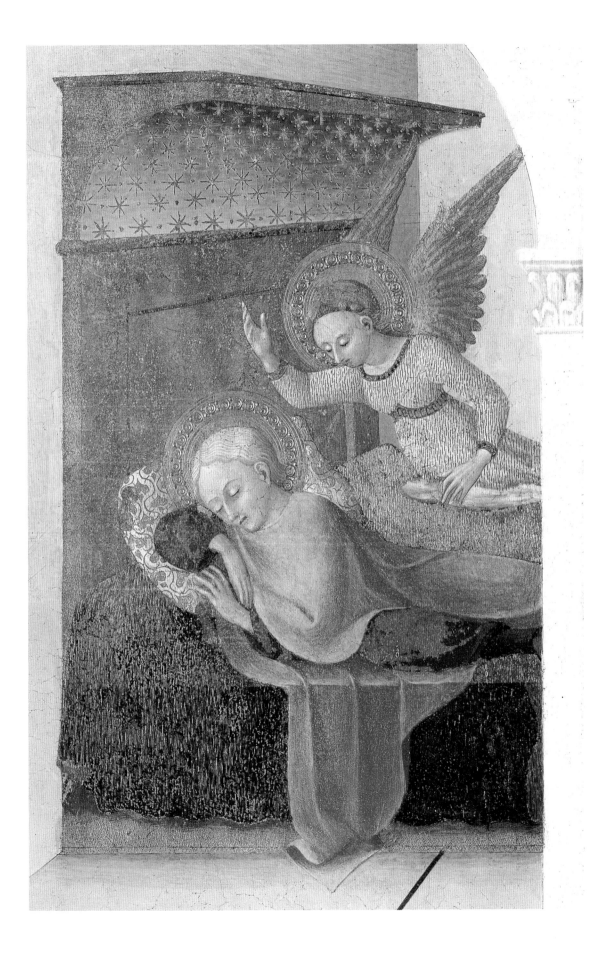

Although separated by fifty years and
five hundred miles these two details
unite with perfect harmony. In each a
young knight is dedicating himself to
some chivalrous ideal. Richard II
kneels to receive a Crusader's banner
from the Virgin; Francis dreams of
the celestial city. This unity of subject
is matched by an equal unity of style,
for both artists derive from the
gentle, courtly Gothicism of the late
fourteenth century, that truly
international style which expressed,
with half-conscious romanticism, the
dying spirit of medieval chivalry. The
Diptych shows this spirit in its
prime. By Sassetta's day it was dead
in the North, killed by civil war,
social and religious anarchy, and
dead in Florence, killed by the fierce
intellectual life of the bourgeoisie.
Only in Siena, incurably old-
fashioned and democratic, was it able
to survive and produce in Sassetta its
most delicate and imaginative
interpreter.

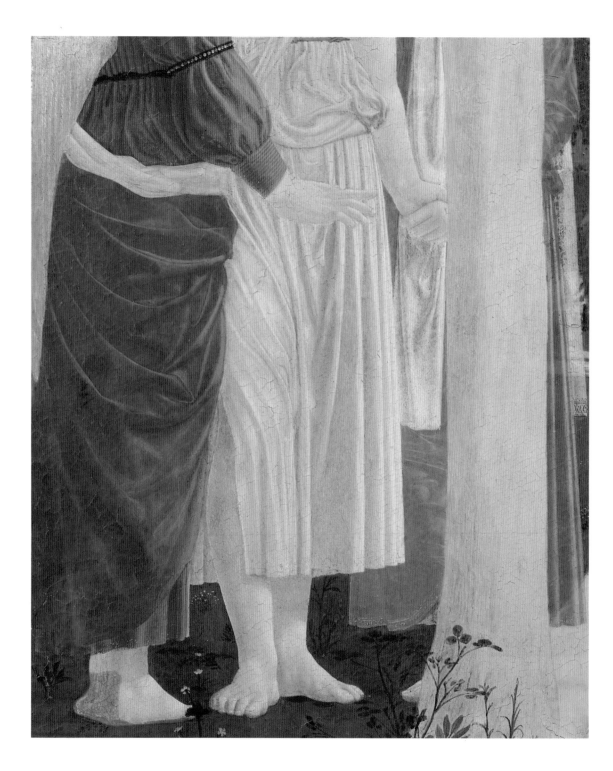

The feet of angels from THE BAPTISM OF CHRIST *by Piero della Francesca, painted about 1450.*

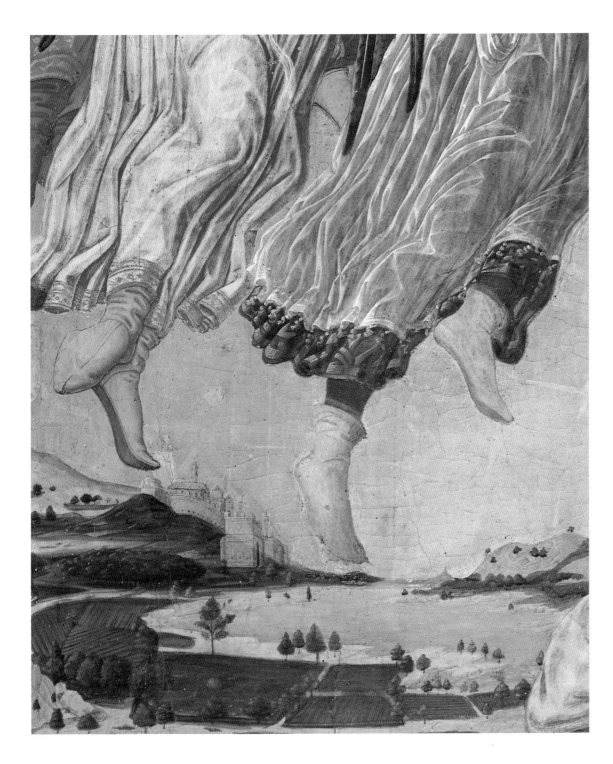

The feet of angels from
**THE ASSUMPTION OF
THE VIRGIN** *by Matteo di
Giovanni, painted about 1474.*

In comparing Piero with his Sienese
contemporaries we are inevitably
reminded of the contrast between
Classical and Gothic architecture,
between the columns of a Greek
temple and the flying buttresses of a
cathedral. In Matteo's *Assumption of
the Virgin*, painted about thirty years
later than Sassetta's Saint Francis
series, the character of the individual
forms is Gothic no longer, but the
movements and silhouettes corres-
pond exactly to those decorative late
Gothic traceries which outside of
Florence and Rome survived almost
to the day when they were
transformed into Baroque.

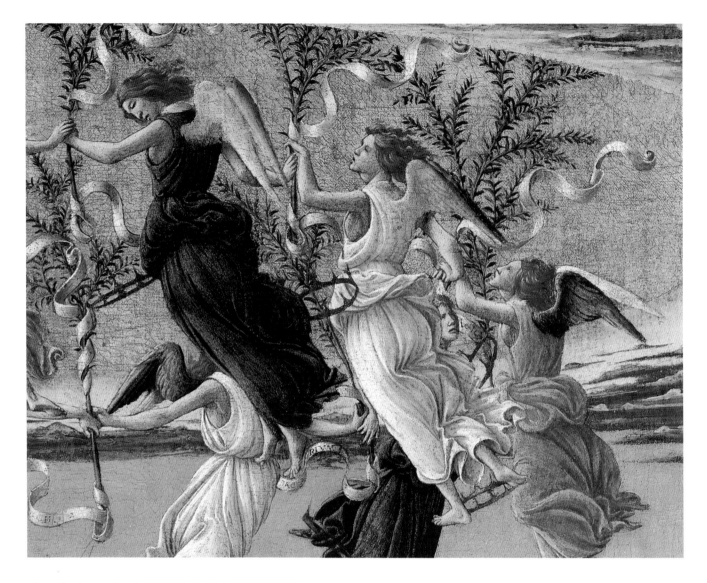

Angels from the MYSTIC NATIVITY *by Botticelli, painted about 1500.*

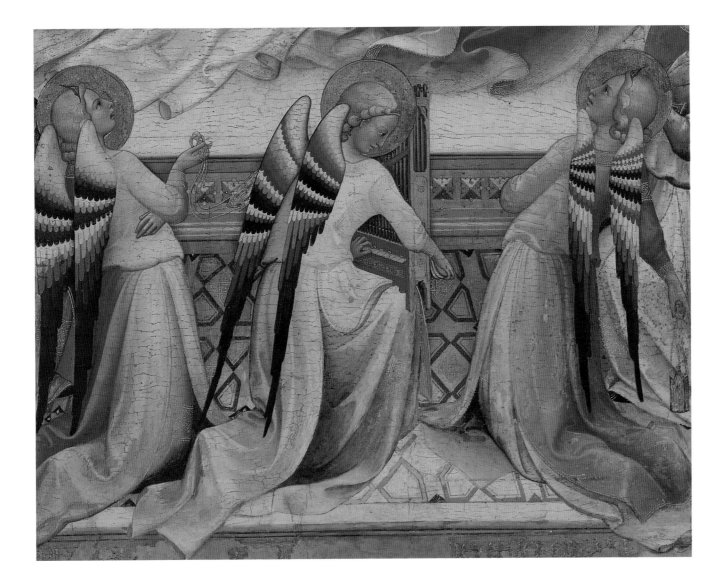

Angels from THE CORONATION OF
THE VIRGIN *by Lorenzo Monaco, painted
about 1415.*

Analogies between music and painting have led to much
loose writing, but everyone can feel some correspondence
between visible lines and the lines of a melody; and
these details admit of restatement in terms of music as
much, perhaps, as anything in European art. We can
follow the main theme rising, falling and being worked
out in variations. In the Botticelli the angels on the far
side of the circle, moving in the opposite direction, give
an extraordinary effect of counterpoint. In the Lorenzo
Monaco the undulating chant is slower, but with some
steep and surprising cadences. In both the melody is set
off by areas of pattern – Lorenzo's diapered floor,
Botticelli's olive branches – which are like a *vibrato*
accompaniment on the strings. How did this lyrical style
come to such perfection in Florence, with its harsh forum
life, practical jokes and Cobdenite morality?[2]

[2] A reference to Richard Cobden, a nineteenth-century statesman
and advocate of free trade.

The Virgin from
**THE ASSUMPTION OF
THE VIRGIN** *by Matteo di
Giovanni, painted about 1474.*

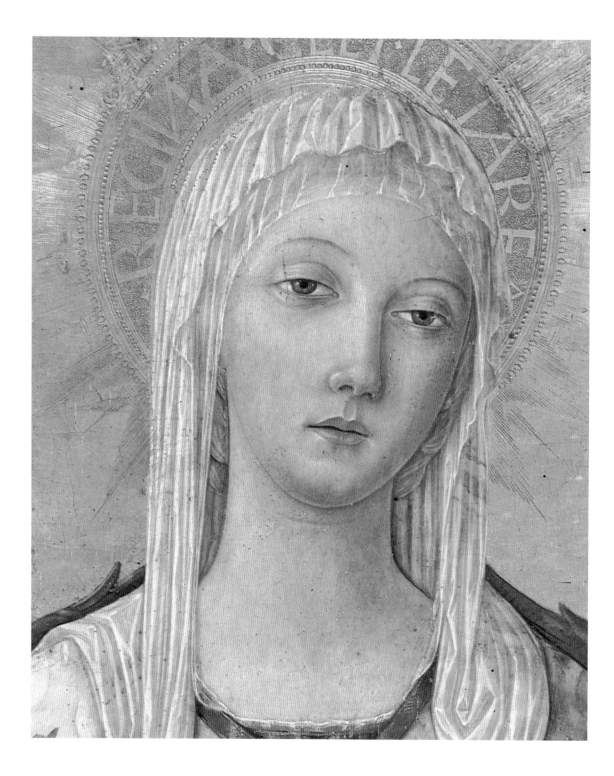

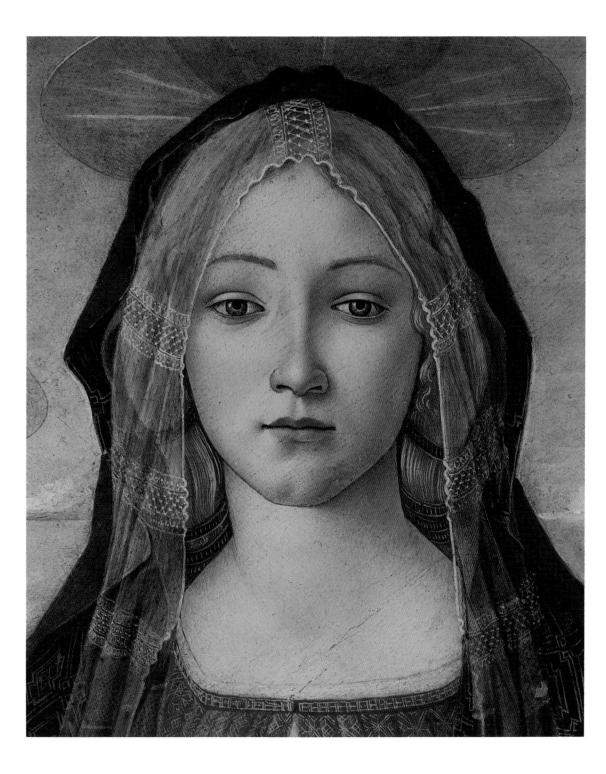

The Virgin from THE VIRGIN AND CHILD WITH SAINT JOHN AND AN ANGEL, *painted in Botticelli's studio, about 1490.*

From Vasari's day onwards art historians have repeated that the serious progressive painting of the fifteenth century was concentrated in Florence, and that Siena was no more than an enchanting backwater. So it is almost a shock to realise that Matteo di Giovanni could conceive a head which from the formal point of view alone is a masterpiece. The outline of the Madonna's face is as simple and momentous as the finest African carving; the concavities of the mask and the elongated eyes also remind us of Negro sculpture. Compared with these large determined arcs, the drawing of the Botticellian Madonna looks very feeble, and we may well ask why for half a century this appealing, but insignificant image should have represented Botticelli in the popular fancy. One answer is that it was almost the first picture of that name to enter the Gallery (in 1855); another, more profound, that the public can only swallow a new style with a copious draught of water, and this Madonna provided just the kind of dilution which was necessary when Botticelli's style was still new and difficult. She is the essential Pre-Raphaelite Madonna, the origin of those wistful maidens in whom Burne-Jones concealed his natural sensuality.

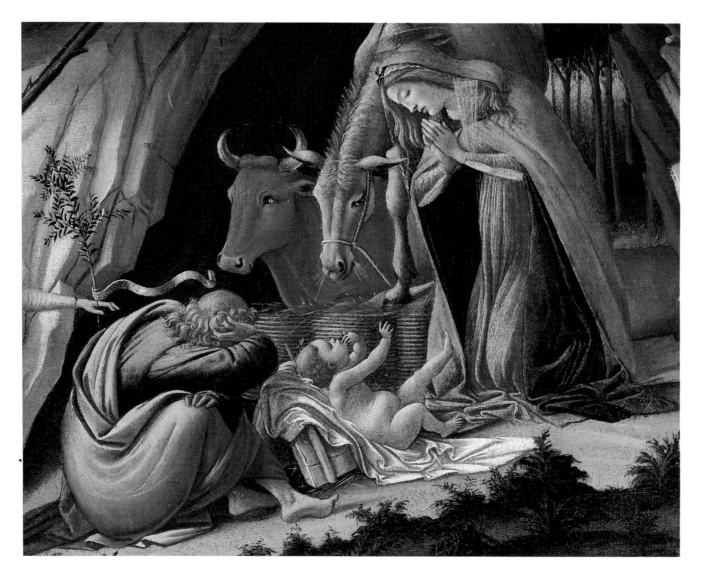

The Holy Family from the MYSTIC
NATIVITY *by Botticelli, painted about 1500.*

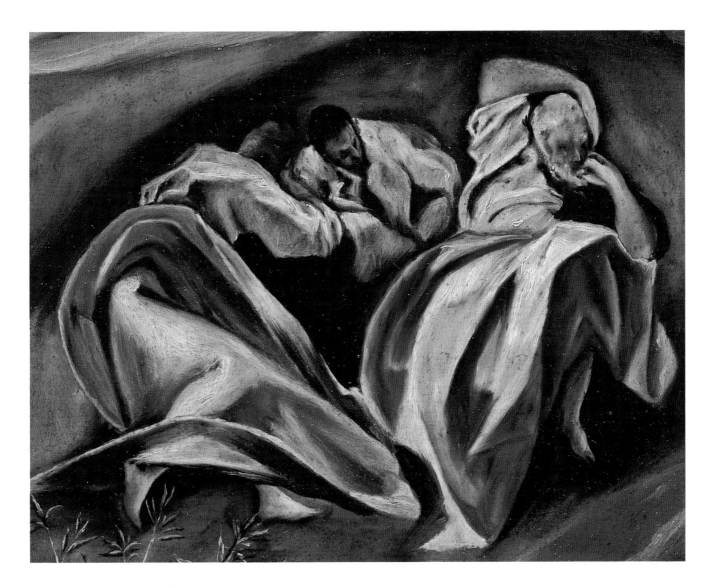

The sleeping Apostles from **THE AGONY IN THE GARDEN**, *painted in El Greco's studio, about 1600.*

Although differing so widely in technique, these two details express the same mood of religious ecstasy in similar language. The figures bend inwards as if under the stress of some magnetic force; their draperies move in large, rapid, unsensuous arcs, or shoot across the scene in harsh diagonals. Naturally, El Greco can move farther from fact. Mannerism – and he may be regarded by those who enjoy a paradox as the greatest Italian Mannerist – allowed a distortion of form never again contemplated until about 1910. But certain details of Botticelli's later work, in particular the Saint Zenobius series, go far towards expressive abstraction. Curiously enough his contemporaries do not seem to have noticed this, and Isabella d'Este's agent in Florence, writing to his mistress in 1502, mentions Botticelli after Perugino and Filippino Lippi as 'an excellent painter and one who works willingly and has no hindrances, as the aforesaid'. In fact, a good man of business; and we are reminded that El Greco, too, organised his genius, so that his studio was almost a factory, supplying the whole of Castille with pictures full of genuine mysticism.

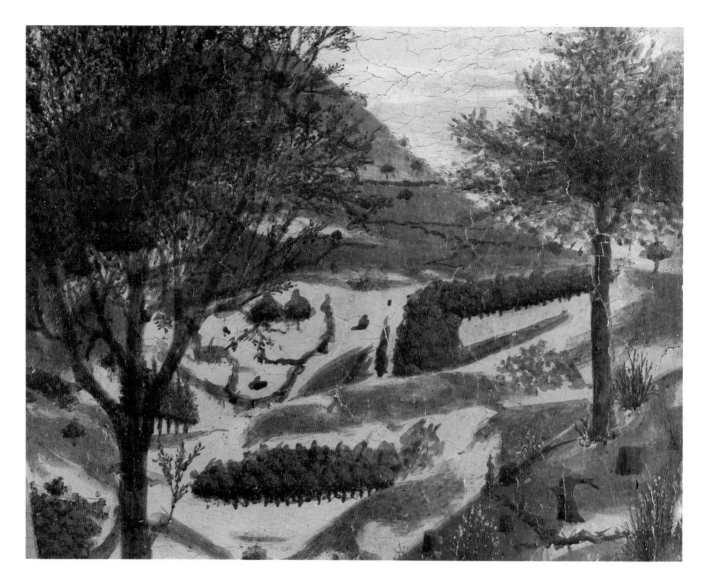

Landscape from THE BAPTISM OF CHRIST *by Piero della Francesca, painted about 1450.*

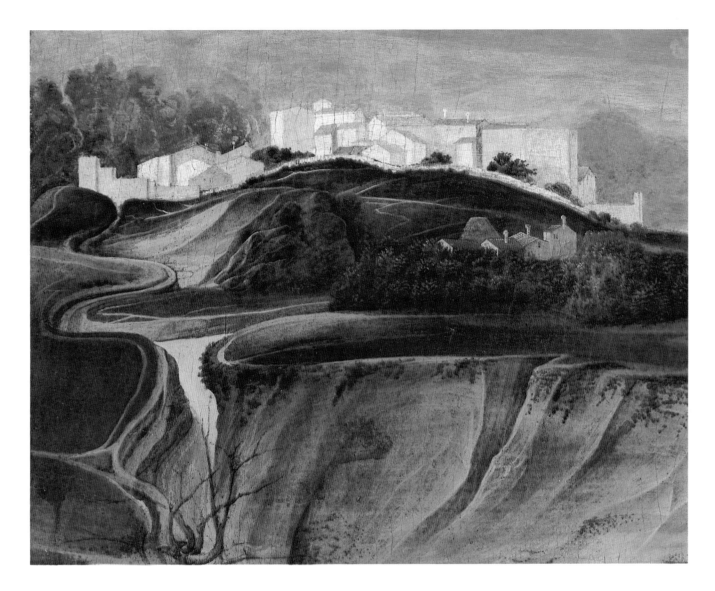

Landscape from THE AGONY IN THE GARDEN *by Giovanni Bellini, painted about 1465.*

Giovanni Bellini was the greatest landscape painter of the fifteenth century. Perugino and the Pollaiuolo brothers, although masters of their respective countrysides, Umbria and the Val d'Arno, lacked his variety. He knew how nature appeared at every hour of the day and season of the year; and was especially fond of the moment of sunset when walled towns and castles on hill-tops catch a light which has already left the plain. It is a moment of great beauty, still to be enjoyed by those who visit Soave, Marostica and others of the few remaining walled towns of the Veneto, and Bellini has used it, without the least exaggeration, to heighten the mood of his most solemn subjects, the Crucifixion or the Agony in the Garden. In this detail the thorny tree, the tortured, winding road and the eventual illumination of the town, seem to symbolise the subject of the picture. But pictorially the landscape needs the sweep of the whole composition and the accents of the figures to give it full value. The background of *The Madonna of the Meadow* (Plate 23) is one of the very few landscapes of the period which do not suffer from isolation.

The landscapes of Piero della Francesca illustrate this fact. Seen in relation to his figures, they are of great importance; isolated they are almost meaningless. Their value lies in the way they sustain the tone of the picture, that still, silvery atmosphere in which Piero's placid divinities perform their noble actions. This detail from *The Baptism* is of great interest, however, as it shows that the calculating Piero was capable of an apparent freedom which recalls the ink landscape paintings of the twelfth-century Southern Sung School, or the work of the drunken Wu-Wei. But unlike the Chinese he is without calligraphic flourish, and for this reason the very blotti-ness of his touch is curiously personal and revealing.

41

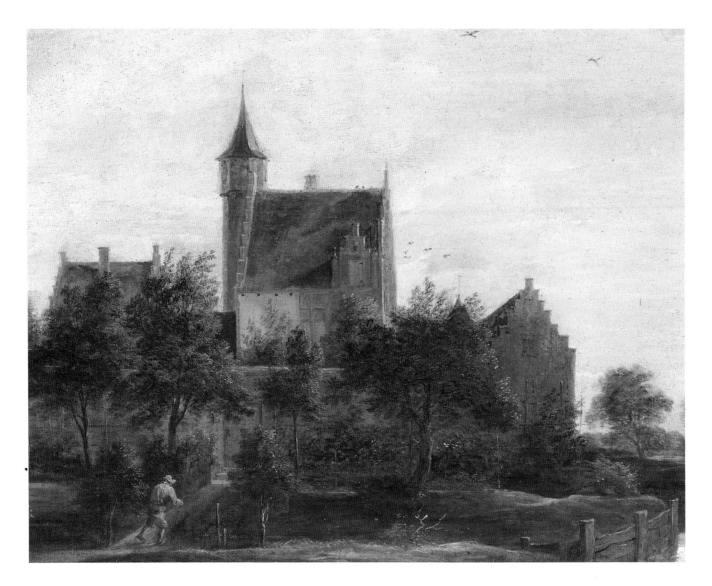

From A VIEW OF HET STERCKSHOF
NEAR ANTWERP *by Teniers the Younger,
painted about 1646.*

Teniers is an underrated landscape painter, because his
figures, though often beautifully painted in themselves,
are never properly related to the background and distract
the eye. When they are inconspicuous, as in *Brick-making*,
at Dulwich Picture Gallery, or when by photography we
are able to see a piece of landscape in isolation, we realise
that he painted nature in rather the same spirit as Sisley
in 1873. He saw the poetry of a prosaic scene and
expressed it with a graceful, sensitive touch. No wonder
he was a favourite painter of the eighteenth-century
English country gentleman, for his backgrounds show
that half-conscious understanding of countryside beauty
which one finds, so differently expressed, in the letters of
Cowper, Cobbett and Edward Fitzgerald.

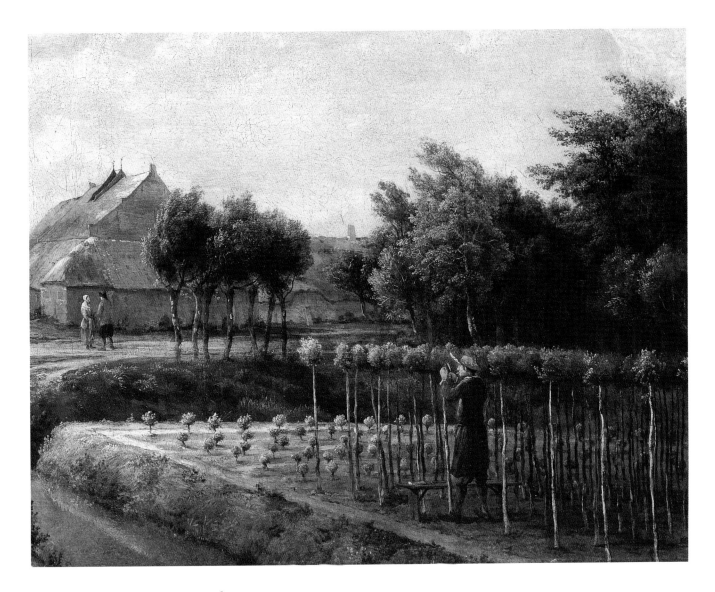

A nurseryman pruning trees from
THE AVENUE, MIDDELHARNIS *by*
Hobbema, painted in 1689.

Although this comes from one of the most familiar
pictures in the Gallery, some people may fail to recognise
it at the first glance, since, in looking at the picture as a
whole, the eye cannot escape shooting down the central
perspective. The idea of making a miniature row of young
trees to accompany and, perhaps, later to supplant the
main avenue is beyond Hobbema's usual powers of
invention. Indeed the whole picture is so far outside his
limited range that eminent Dutch critics have doubted
its authenticity, and ascribed it, to my mind quite
unconvincingly, to a pasticheur named van Kessell.

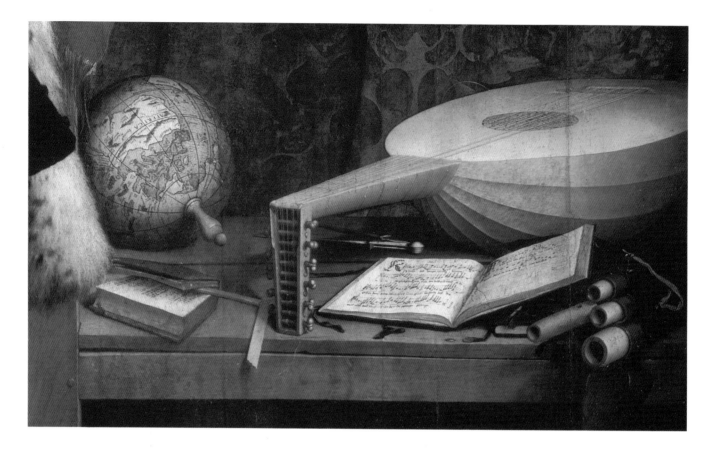

Still life from THE AMBASSADORS *by Holbein, painted in 1533.*

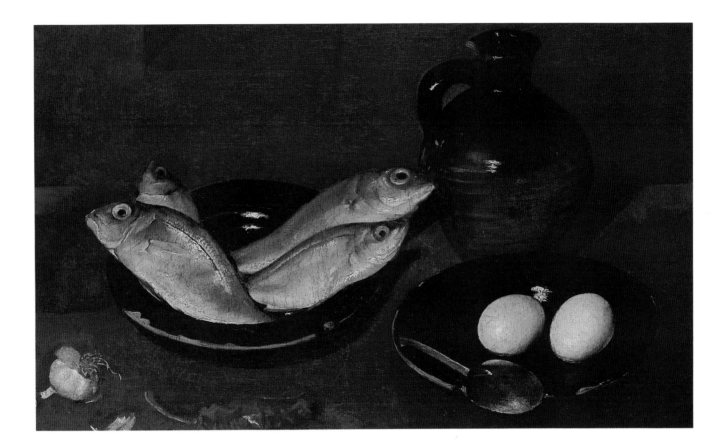

Still life from **CHRIST IN THE HOUSE OF MARTHA AND MARY** *by Velázquez, painted in 1618.*

These two details show two distinct ways in which still life can be made a subject for painting. It may provide the painter with a sort of intellectual game, allied to geometry or counterpoint, in which the winner is he who can combine the most ingenious variety of shapes in two and three dimensions. This is the motif of the earliest piece of post-classical still life known to me, a painting in the Arena Chapel, Padua, presumably by Giotto, which seems to represent a birdcage. This stage of still life found its fullest expression in the marvellous inlaid woodwork done all over Italy during the Renaissance, much of which was designed by great artists like Baldovinetti and even Piero della Francesca. The geometrical basis of such designs was systematised by Piero's pupil, Pacioli, in his *Divina Proportione*: but there was also a literary element. Certain objects were included on account of their symbolical or evocative qualities. Holbein's still life, in spite of its realism, belongs to this tradition. He even uses the favourite properties of *intarsiatori*, a lute, a globe, open books, geometrical instruments; but the tradition is already waning and the direct impact of design is weakened by over-realistic detail.

With Velázquez another tradition of still life, originated in part by Caravaggio some twenty-five years earlier, is well established. The artist paints inanimate objects primarily because they keep still. Only thus can he give himself up without distraction to rendering in paint the exact shape, substance and texture of what he sees. Of course, the objects themselves may be arranged in such a way as to form an architectural composition, and may be used to reveal almost the whole range of a painter's sensibility; but the underlying motive is realism. This detail from Velázquez, then, is the ancestor of Chardin, Bonvin, Manet and, from one point of view, Cézanne. Yet Cézanne led to Cubism, and early Cubism is certainly a return to the still life of the *intarsiatori*. How curious that musical instruments, printed pages and all the old paraphernalia should have reappeared, though the Cubists did not bother to paint each letter on a page, as Holbein has done, but very sensibly gummed pieces of newspaper straight on to the canvas.

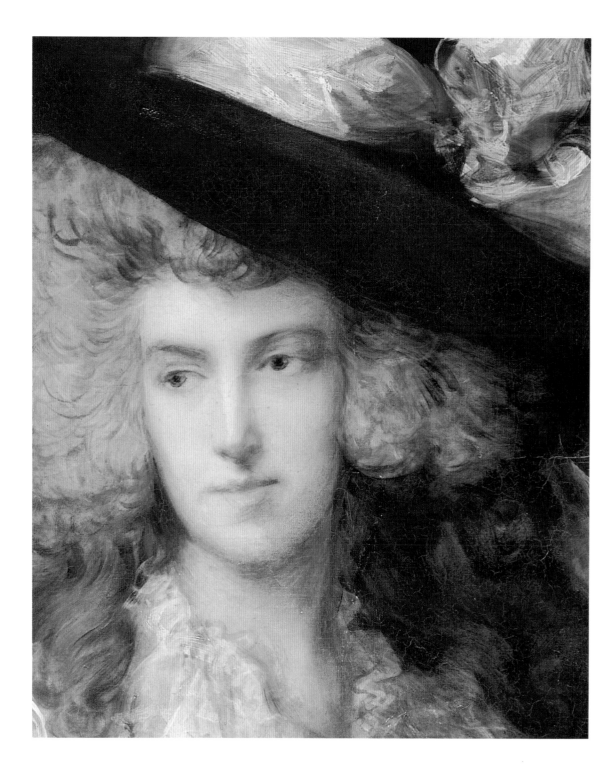

46

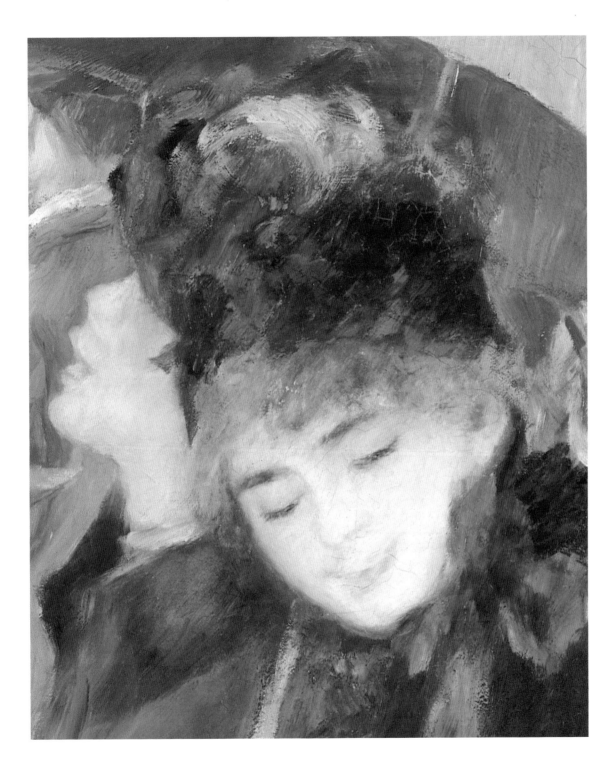

The likeness between Gainsborough and Renoir is familiar to all amateurs, and far more telling examples could be found outside the Gallery; indeed, these details show the essential difference between them. This may be expressed by the story in Smith's *Nollekens and his Times* (1829), of how Gainsborough, receiving a letter in a beautiful hand, pinned it on his easel as an inspiration; whereas Renoir was so little dependent on graceful execution that he painted some of his greatest pictures when, crippled with rheumatism, his brush had to be strapped to his hand. He even created some of his admirable sculpture without touching the clay, simply by pointing with a stick. One cannot imagine Gainsborough producing sculpture at all, and without his handling much of his work would melt away. The girl from *Les Parapluies*, though kept down in tone to the level of the whole composition, has an amplitude which implies a fuller grasp of form.

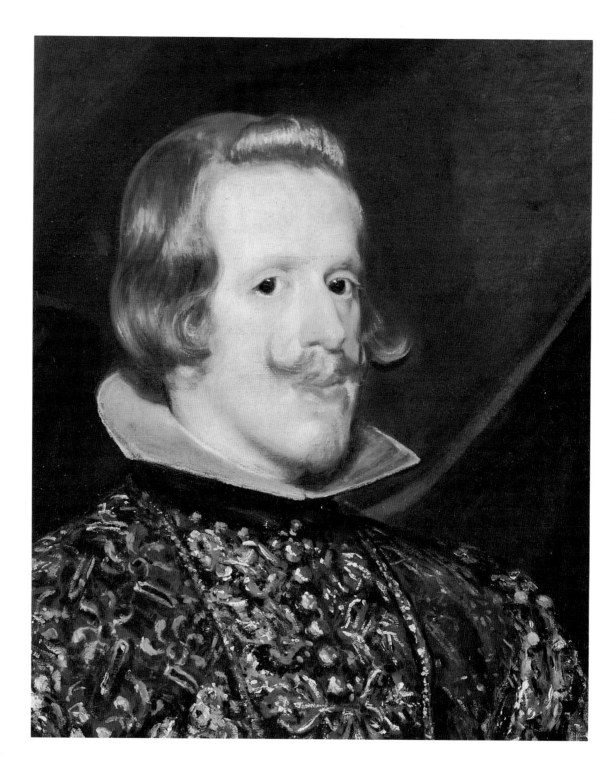

From **PHILIP IV OF SPAIN** *by Velázquez, painted in the mid-1630s.*

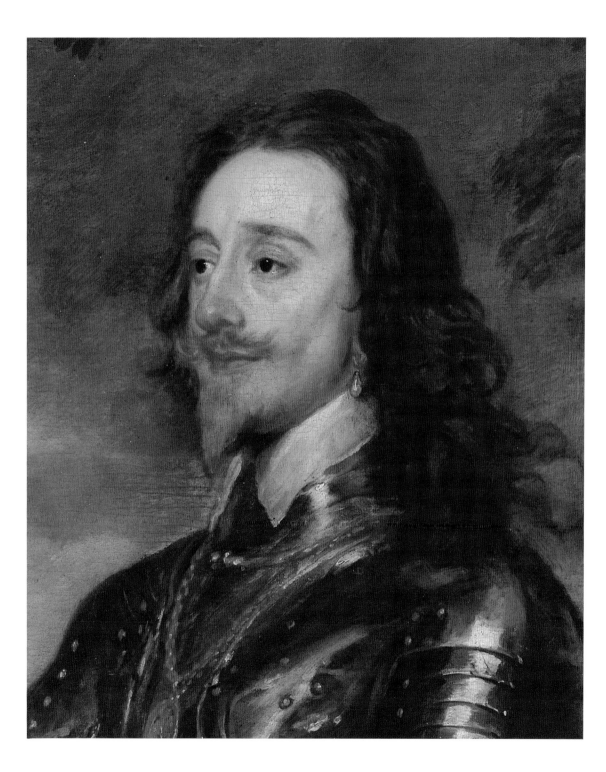

From EQUESTRIAN PORTRAIT OF CHARLES I *by van Dyck, painted about 1638.*

By comparing these two heads of kings, painted perhaps in the same year, we can realise the characters of the two great Court limners of the period. No one doubts that Velázquez was the greater artist, but the portrait of Philip IV of Spain, painted as a display of brilliant handling, does not do justice to his finest qualities. The head of Charles I, on the other hand, shows van Dyck at his best, and at first sight looks solider than its neighbour. This is partly due to photography, which always flatters pictures painted in glazes over monochrome foundation at the expense of direct painting in colour. What survives photography, however, is Velázquez's detached vision. Philip IV looked like that. Charles I wanted to look like that, and van Dyck has subtly interpreted his sitter's romantic egotism. That is the aim of every fashionable portrait painter; and today no one who is devoid of this gift can hope to make more than a bare livelihood out of the art of painting.

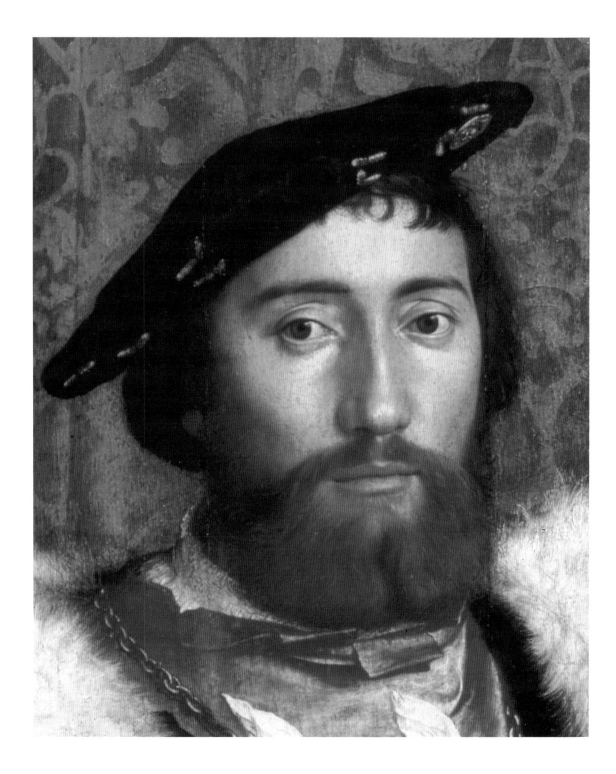

Jean de Dinteville from
THE AMBASSADORS
by Holbein, painted in 1533.

50

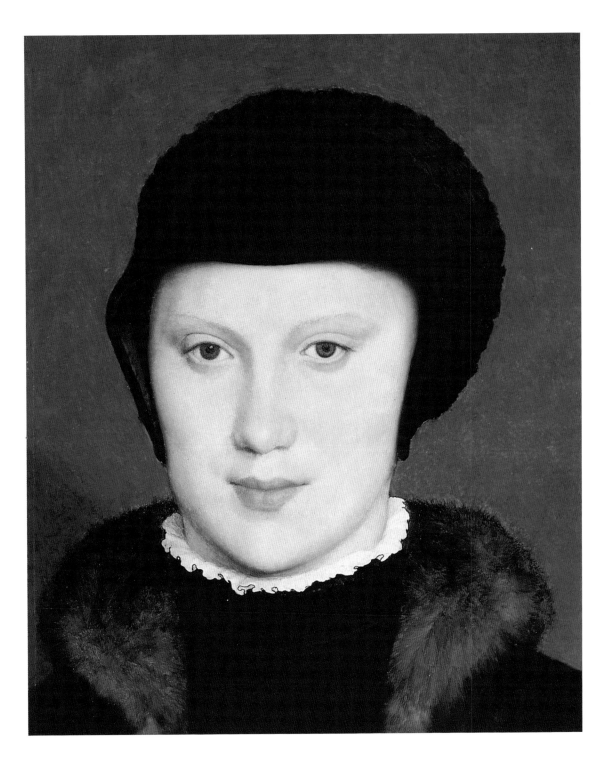

From **CHRISTINA OF DENMARK, DUCHESS OF MILAN** *by Holbein, painted about 1538.*

Photographic details may help to redress our scale of values. *'The Ambassadors'* is a large panel, full of distracting properties, and we fail to realise that the heads are among the masterpieces of Holbein's portraiture. They are also well preserved, whereas poor Christina has suffered considerably. Her cheeks are covered with retouches, and her left eye is almost entirely gone over.[3] This is clear when we compare the photograph of her head with the plate opposite, but in the original the simplicity and concentration of the whole design are so effective that we are not too critical of such details, and see her as what she once was – the most moving of all Holbein's larger portraits.

[3] Some of the retouching has been removed by subsequent cleaning.

51

MADAME MOITESSIER
by Ingres, begun in 1844, completed in 1857.

Madame Moitessier was a famous beauty. That is an aspect of the subject which it is difficult for us to realise – difficult, but essential, for Ingres felt it acutely and made it the basis of his design. She represents beauty enthroned, like a Phoenician goddess, half Roman, half Oriental, calmly aware of her feminine potency. Contemporary taste seems to find this self-confidence irritating, and the head which Ingres referred to as *terrible et belle*, repulsive. Even her hand, which delighted the critic and writer Gautier, has been abused for its lack of bony structure. By 1856 Ingres had been acclaimed for forty years as the greatest draughtsman in Europe; none of his contemporaries had been so foolish as to say that his hands were 'out of drawing', and we must, I fear, conclude that a sense of plastic coherency is less common now than it was in that derided epoch of taste, the mid-nineteenth century. For whatever we may think of her as a beauty, Madame Moitessier is a masterpiece of formal construction. There is a largeness and continuity in every sequence of form which makes her neighbours look haphazard, and apparent defects of painting spring from deliberate subordination to a central idea.

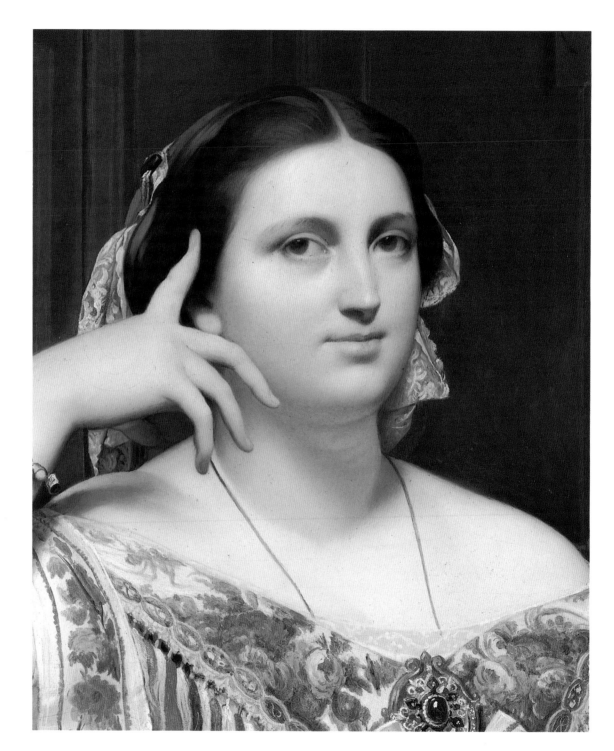

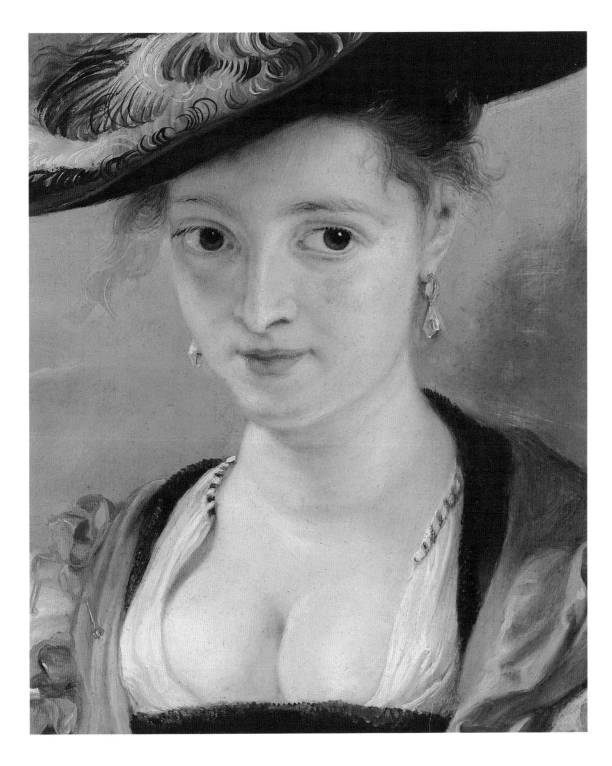

Susanna Lunden from LE CHAPEAU DE PAILLE *by Rubens, painted about 1622–5.*

This is a study of the contrast between Susanna Lunden's delicate complexion and her dark eyes; and to give this contrast its full effect Rubens has painted her under a hat the tone of her eyes, with her face lit by reflected light, so that all dark shadows are eliminated, leaving only the local colours of lips, eyebrows and iris. Illumination by reflected light usually means rather flat painting, but Rubens has been able to keep the modelling alive at every point with a delicacy and transparency which is his secret, and with such apparent ease that we think more of his enchanting sitter than of his superb technical skill.

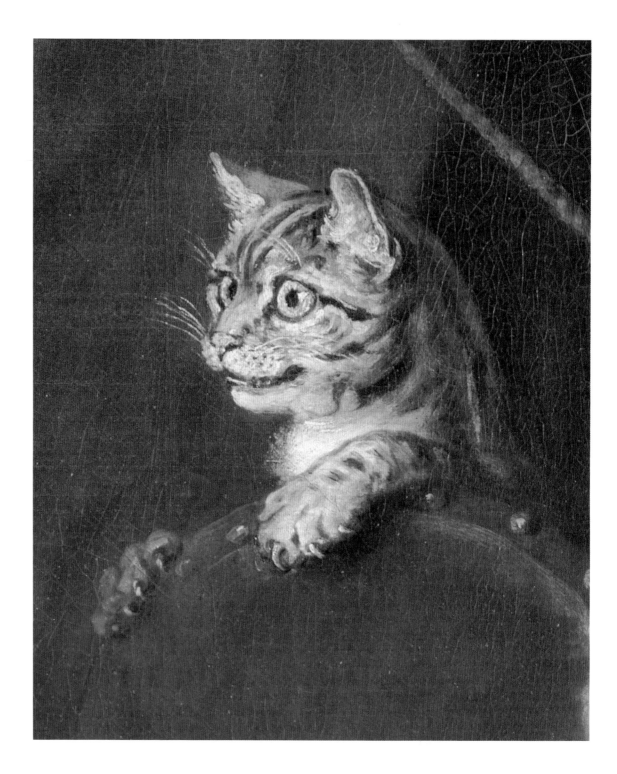

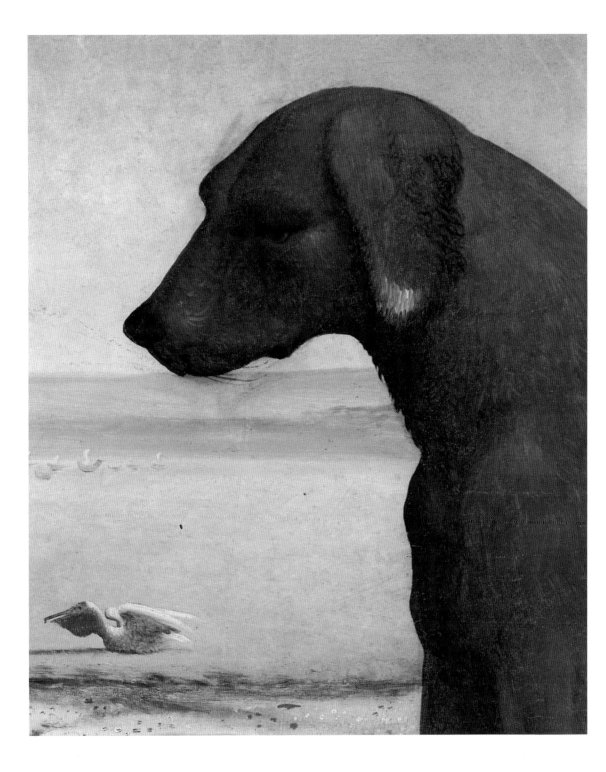

A dog from
**A MYTHOLOGICAL
SUBJECT** *by Piero di Cosimo,
painted about 1500.*

Hogarth enjoyed painting this cat so
much that the Graham children look
hollow and lifeless beside her. She is
the embodiment of cockney vitality,
alert and adventurous – a sort of Nell
Gwynn among cats. Her vulgarity
would hardly be noticeable, were
she not confronted by the noble
silhouette of Piero's hound who
regards her with the gravity of an
antique philosopher. The novelist
Paul Bourget, when asked what the
English critic Walter Pater looked
like, replied: 'Il ressemblait à un
amant de Circe transformé en dogue.'

55

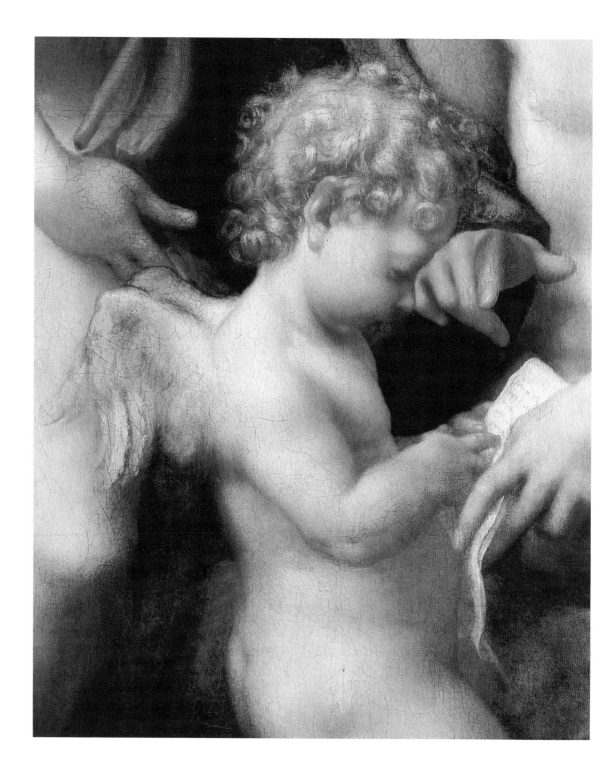

Cupid from THE SCHOOL OF LOVE *by Correggio, painted in the mid-1520s.*

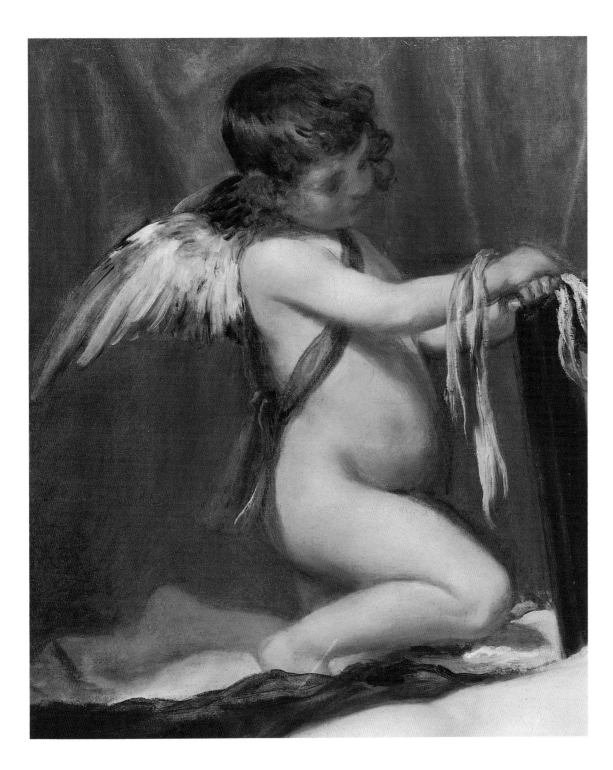

Cupid from THE ROKEBY VENUS *by Velázquez, painted about 1648–51.*

Similarity of subject makes clear the great difference in handling. Correggio, in spite of his love of softness, begins from definition by drawing. The forms are modelled and then glazed. Velázquez has also used glazes in the flesh parts; but his Cupid's head, hair and wings are painted with a directness which no sixteenth-century painter, except perhaps Tintoretto, would have considered decent; and the Cupid's left leg would have shocked Correggio, though it may be compared to the left hand of Tintoretto's princess on Plate 66.

57

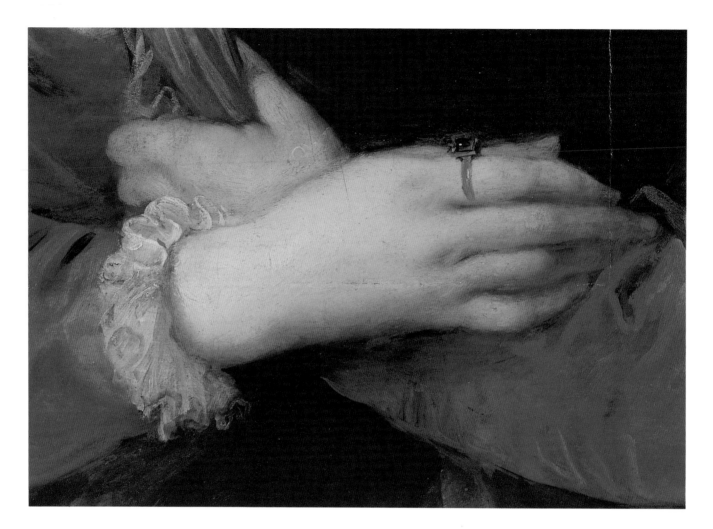

Hands from LE CHAPEAU DE PAILLE *by
Rubens, painted about 1622–5.*

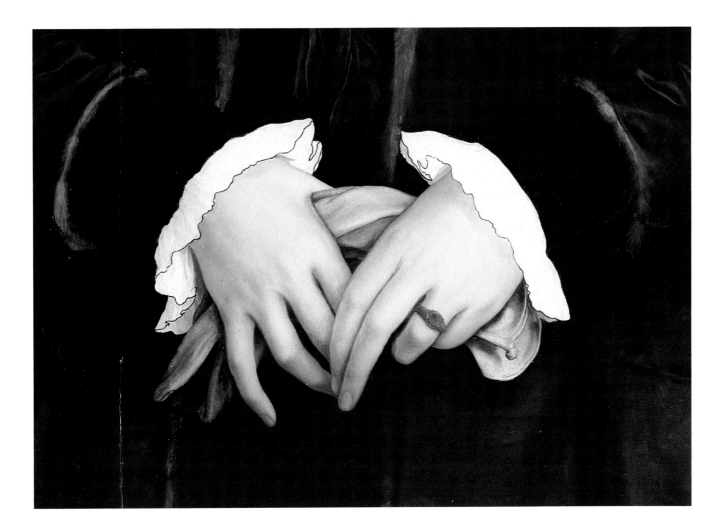

Hands from CHRISTINA OF DENMARK,
DUCHESS OF MILAN *by Holbein, painted
about 1538.*

These hands illustrate the Renaissance and Baroque
principles of composition. Behind Holbein's conception is
an enclosed geometrical form like a pyramid. Rubens is
thinking of an undulating landscape.

How perfectly *dix-huitième* Correggio was! This detail should have been placed opposite a Nattier, if there had been a suitable one in the Gallery. There is something disconcerting about an artist who belongs so completely to an epoch other than his own. Any work of art must vibrate in the memory, but the resonances of a Correggio are so insistent and unexpected that our true sense of values is distracted. Before we have had time to look at his pictures for their own sakes we have begun mentally to relate them to the stylistic development of the seven-teenth and eighteenth centuries. If it could be established that Correggio, like 'Ercole Grandi', was the invention of some early art historian, and that all his pictures were painted at a later date, how should we value him? I think we should say that he was the greatest painter of the eighteenth century, with a wider range than Watteau, a finer sense of beauty than Boucher, and a solider core than Fragonard.

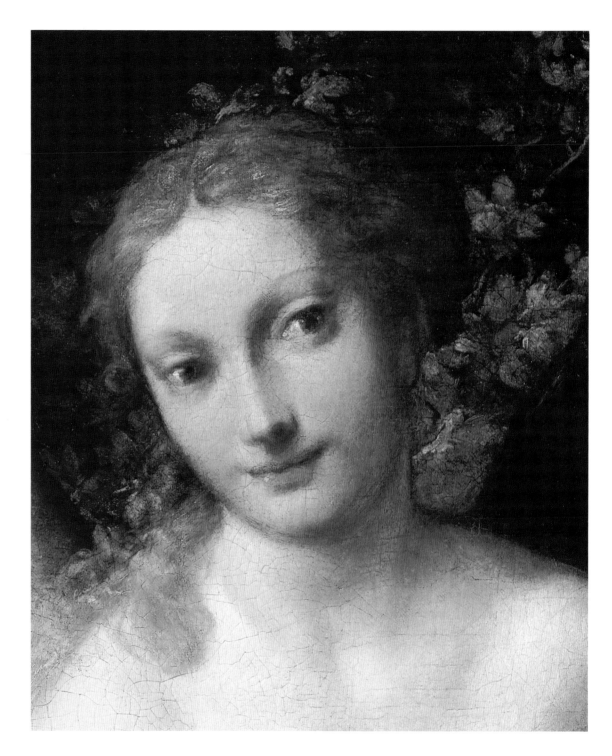

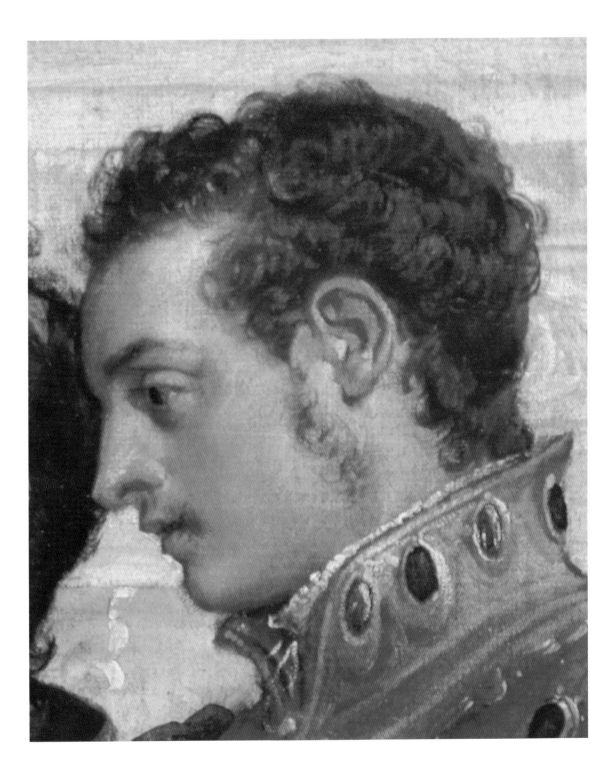

Alexander from THE FAMILY OF DARIUS BEFORE ALEXANDER *by Veronese, painted in the 1570s.*

It is typical of Veronese's lack of interest in drama (see note to Plate 18) that he should have made no attempt to recreate the historical Alexander – still less, it will be remembered, the family of Darius. His subject is a young Venetian model, painted with a breadth and directness which looks the more striking by contrast with the feminine subtleties of Correggio. A hundred years earlier Mantegna would have ransacked his friends' collections for coins, gems, and reliefs which might give him a correct idea of Alexander's appearance. This archaeological enthusiasm died out of painting early in the sixteenth century, but still survived in architecture, thanks to the authority of the Roman architect Vitruvius; and the backgrounds of Veronese's pictures contain examples of High Renaissance architecture freer and more imaginative than those actually constructed.

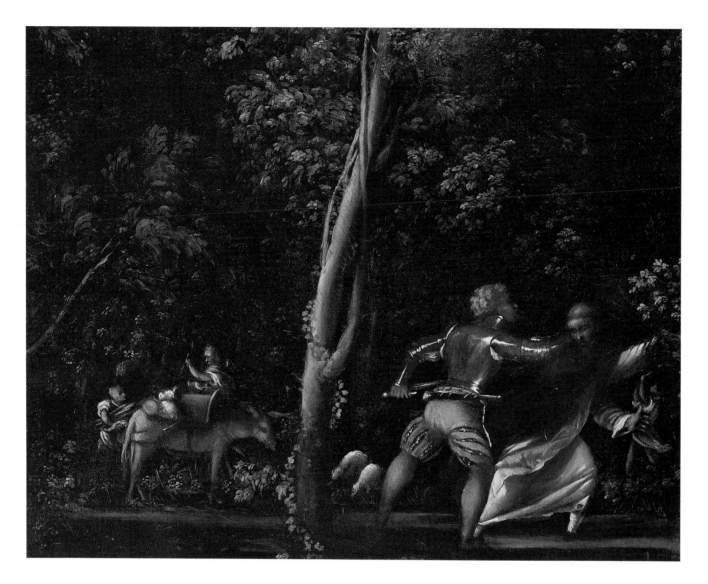

From THE DEATH OF SAINT PETER
MARTYR, *ascribed to Bernardino da Asola,
painted in the 1540s.*

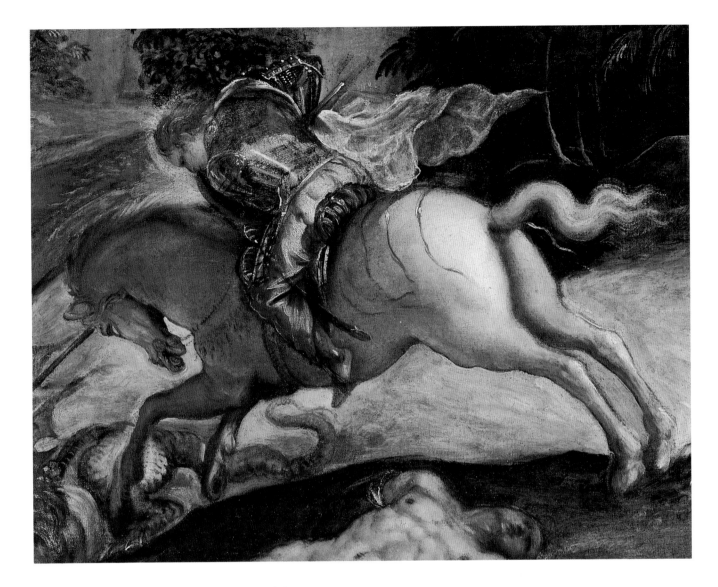

From SAINT GEORGE AND THE DRAGON *by Tintoretto, painted in the 1550s or 1560s.*

It is a proof of the rapid growth of Venetian romanticism under Giorgione's influence that a detail from Bernardino da Asola goes well enough opposite Tintoretto's Saint George. A detail from Bellini's picture of the same subject (*The Assassination of Saint Peter Martyr*, around 1500), which is also in the Gallery, would look quite set and Quattrocento. So strong was the influence of this romantic mood in Venice that, like Raphael's classicism in Rome, it was the subject of a series of revivals throughout the sixteenth century, thus producing the many hundreds of pictures formerly labelled 'Giorgione',

under which name, in fact, the Bernardino passed into the Gallery in 1831. There is nothing in Italian art more romantic than Tintoretto's Saint George. Even the knights and Moroccans of Delacroix look relatively prosaic beside him, because Delacroix never allowed himself such extravagant effects of illumination. We have to look for parallels in non-Mediterranean painting – in Altdorfer's *Battle of Alexander* (Alte Pinakothek, Munich), or in Turner's *Ulysses deriding Polyphemus* in the National Gallery.

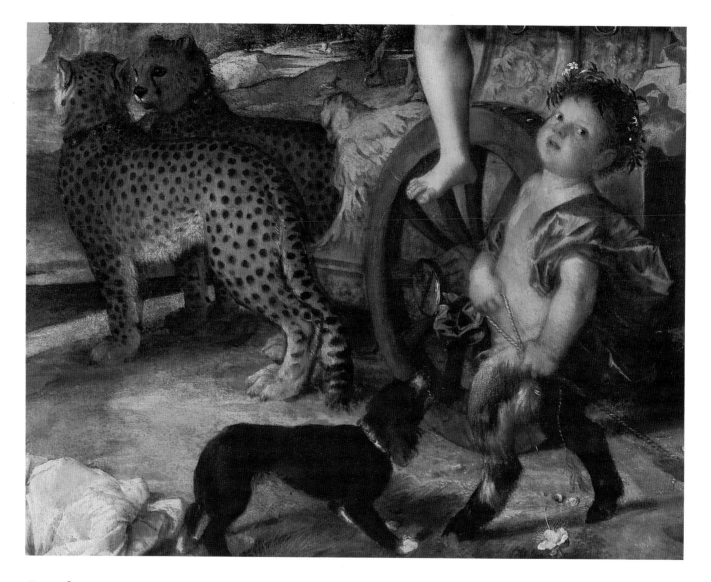

Satyr from BACCHUS AND ARIADNE *by Titian, painted in 1522–3.*

The baby satyr is one of the most charming inhabitants of the National Gallery; but how much of him is original? Until the discoloured varnish has been removed it is impossible to know, and personally I do not think the knowledge worth the appalling risks involved. We can guess by analogy with Titian's other Bacchanals that the *Bacchus and Ariadne* must be covered with minor damages, but these are well concealed by ancient retouchings and a dark, golden varnish; although the general tone of the picture must be very different from what it was in Titian's lifetime, it has a unity and richness which cleaning would almost certainly destroy.[4]

[4] The thick yellow varnish was in fact removed during cleaning in 1969, uncovering some damage but revealing Titian's gloriously vivid colours.

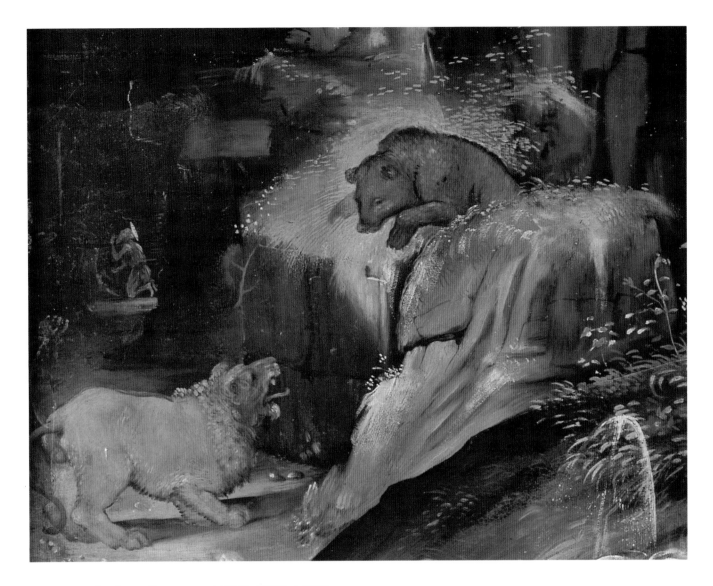

A lion and a bear from THE VIRGIN AND
CHILD WITH SAINTS JEROME AND
DOMINIC *by Filippino Lippi, painted
about 1485.*

Even those who know the Gallery well may not have
recognised the source of this amusing detail, which
reminds us more of Piero di Cosimo than Filippino. By
selecting such passages as these the camera can show us
how much fantasy and invention the Renaissance artists
were forced, by the serious nature of their commissions,
to squeeze into their backgrounds, or to express in
ephemeral decorations, pageants and masquerades now
completely lost to us.

The Princess from SAINT GEORGE AND THE DRAGON *by Tintoretto, painted in the 1550s or 1560s.*

No opening in the book is less in need of comment; or rather any useful comment would have to fill a volume, for it would turn into an answer to the question how artists came to give unity, movement and colour to their subjects by the convention of flying draperies. In art we are so used to voluminous draperies, fluttering in a wind which often fails to disturb the surrounding foliage, that we forget how uncommonly this happens in life. It is, of course, a convention of Greek art, found as early as the fourth-century BC Mausoleum and the Nereid monument, but owing its diffusion to the innumerable sarcophagi which derived in style from the Pergamene school. These sarcophagi were the chief sources of Classical art known to the Middle Ages and the early Renaissance; but in addition fluttering draperies must have been common in the illustrations to Classical manuscripts, and thence they were transposed into the ninth-century Utrecht psalter and its numerous derivatives; thus they influenced such pieces of pure Romanesque sculpture as the prophets of Moissac (the abbey-church of St Pierre), which were generally taken from manuscript illustrations. This takes us a long way from Bacchus, but he is not so far from the Hellenistic sarcophagi, and we can understand why this convention had such authority in the Renaissance. What a magnificent pictorial convention it was, allowing a painter to unite two groups with a flood of moving colour and to put a great splash of white or crimson

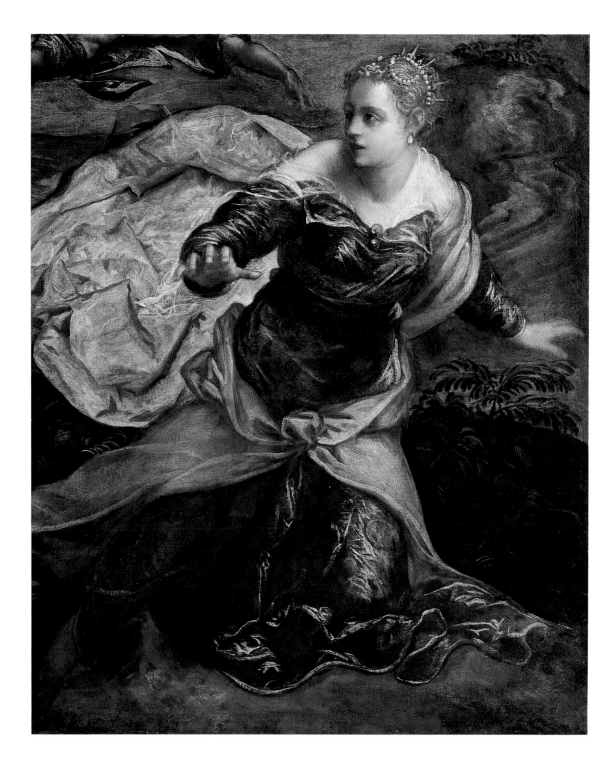

66

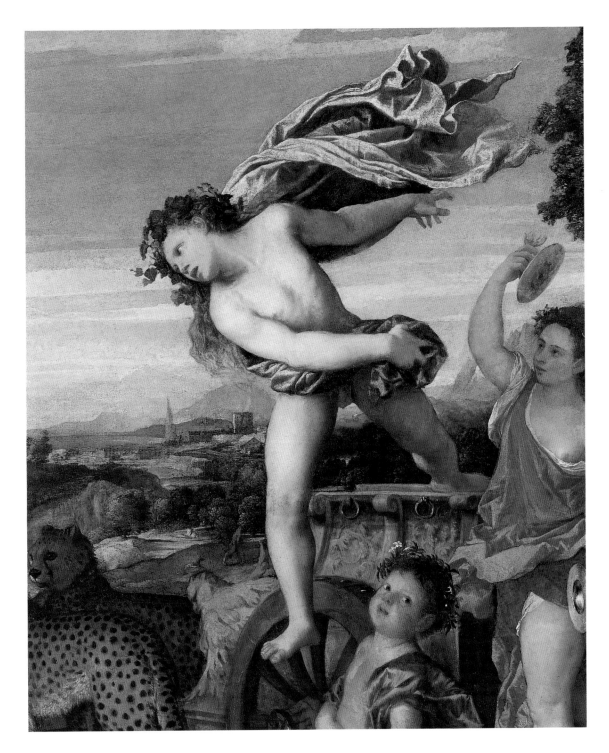

Continued
against a blue sky. He could frame a head, and hide an awkward plane, and keep a dull passage alive: in fact, flowing drapery was almost as useful to the Italian of the sixteenth and seventeenth centuries as cloud to the Chinese landscape painter of the Sung and Yuan dynasties. No wonder this invaluable means became an end in itself, so that in Bernini and the Baroque painters drapery is all. In this detail and elsewhere Tintoretto shows us how far the convention can be ridden without its taking the bit between its teeth. He always subordinates drapery to the design as a whole, and the vitality of his handling prevents it from ever having the mere windiness of Pozzo or Pietro da Cortona.

The young Bronzino from
**JOSEPH WITH JACOB
IN EGYPT** *by Pontormo,
painted about 1515.*

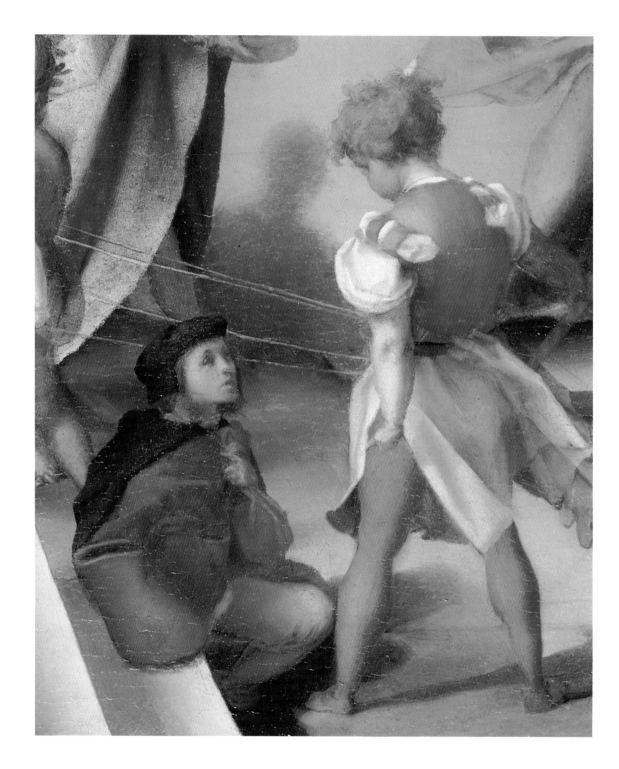

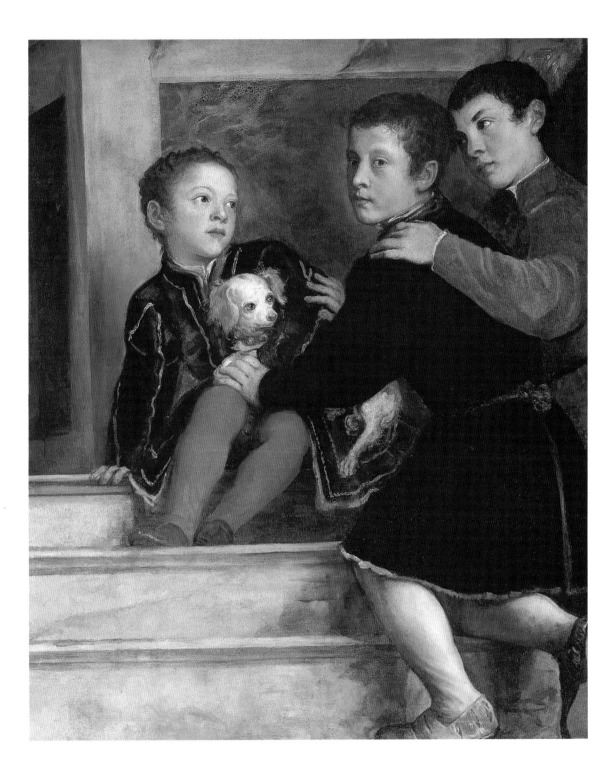

The children of Andrea Vendramin from **THE VENDRAMIN FAMILY** *by Titian, begun about 1543.*

These two sets of children show the nervous, sentimental elaboration of Florentine painting in its decline and the robust materialism of Venetian painting at its zenith. Only in the Titian the boy with the dog is slightly romanticised and perhaps was worked on by van Dyck, to whom the picture once belonged.[5] In his description of the Pontormo, Vasari tells us that the little boy on the steps is the young Bronzino; and as Vasari was a great admirer of the picture and knew Bronzino well personally, this is certainly correct. He entered Pontormo's studio at an early age, and in the picture can hardly be more than twelve years old. This would mean that Pontormo was about twenty-one when he painted it, but he has already evolved his curious, intricate, personal style. He was, in fact, one of the most precocious of Italian painters, with the usual result that his later work suffers from a kind of fastidious exhaustion.

[5] Van Dyck owned the painting from approximately 1636 until his death in 1641. He is unlikely to have worked on it as Kenneth Clark suggests.

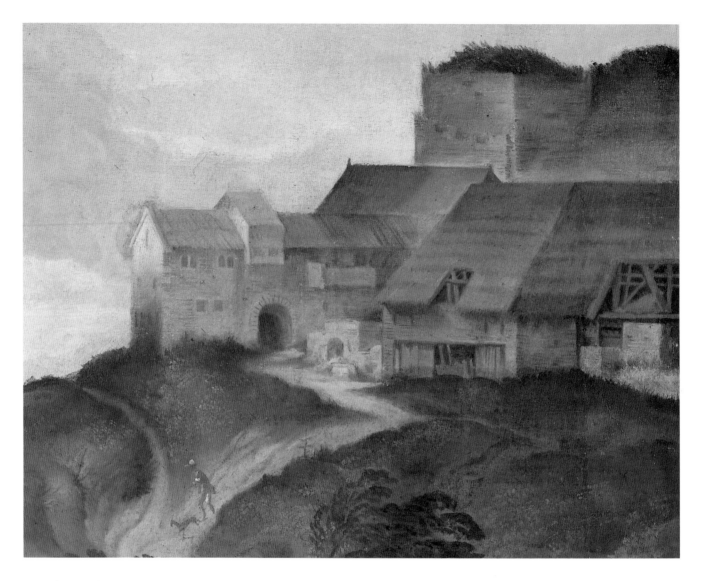

Landscape from NOLI ME TANGERE *by Titian, painted about 1510.*

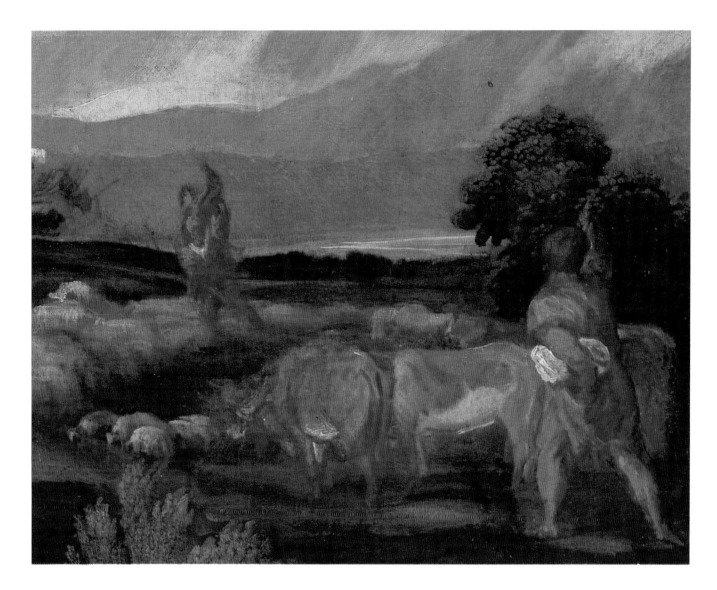

Landscape from
MADONNA AND CHILD WITH SAINTS
by Titian, painted in the 1530s.

The group of buildings in Plate 70 should be famous in the history of landscape painting for it occurs, in almost identical form, in Giorgione's *Sleeping Venus* (Gemälde-galerie, Dresden), and reversed in Titian's *Sacred and Profane Love* (Villa Borghese, Rome). Of these versions, that in the background of the National Gallery's '*Noli me Tangere*' is by far the most delicately painted, and I am inclined to accept the hypothesis recently put forward that it and other parts of the picture are from the hand of Giorgione.[6] Paradoxically enough, the version in the Dresden *Venus* seems to be by Titian who, the contemporary critic Michiel tells us, finished the picture. This is an occasion when a question of connoisseurship is worth considering; for the inventor of this lovely motif must be

reckoned one of the great prophets of landscape painting. Who else, besides Rembrandt, has achieved this combination of architectural grandeur and atmosphere, mystery and peace?

The detail on the opposite page looks coarse and clumsy by comparison. From the photograph we may even doubt if it is by Titian, but the original shows an observation of nature expressed with great force of colour which is convincing.

[6] This 1934 attribution to Giorgione is now considered to be without justification.

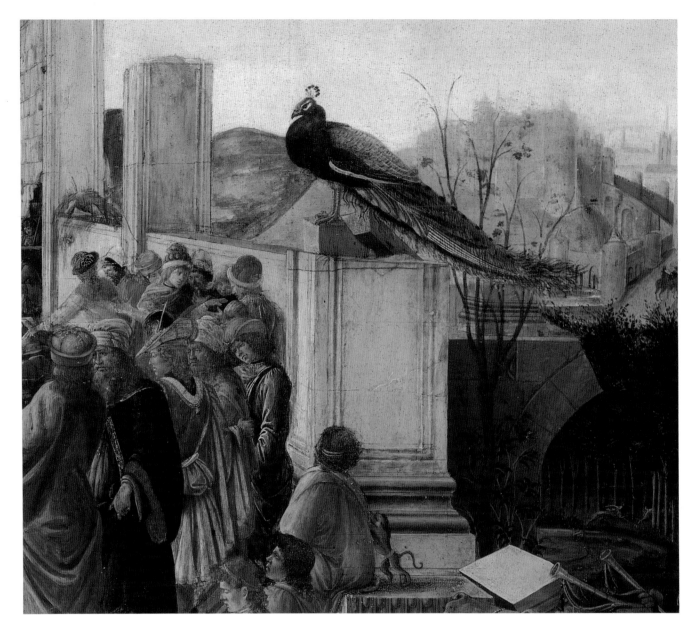

From THE ADORATION OF THE KINGS
by Botticelli, painted about 1475.

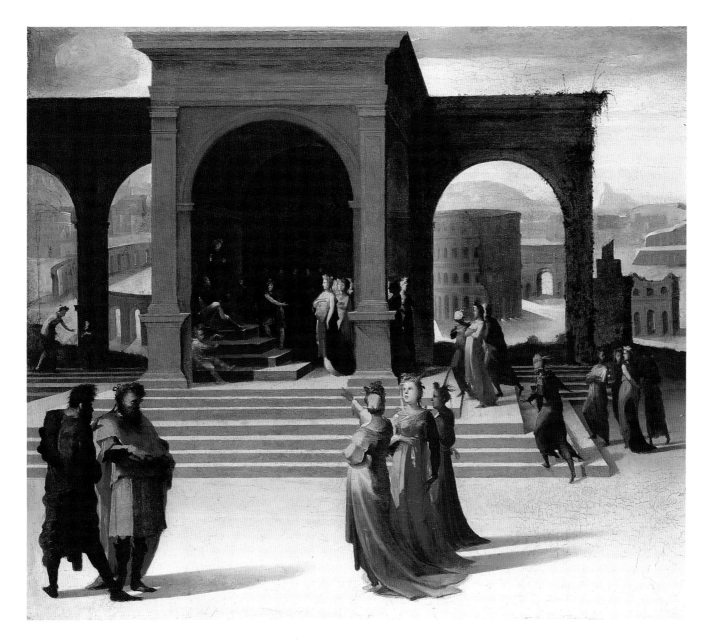

From AN UNIDENTIFIED SCENE *by Beccafumi, painted about 1440–5.*

The round arches and emphatic verticals in the Beccafumi are echoed in the Botticelli; even the sweeping dresses of the women find a much amplified counterpart in Botticelli's peacock. Beccafumi is an underrated artist. With his lively handling and quick eye for an amusing silhouette he is the ancestor of Guardi, Callot and Sickert, and shares their love of artificial light. Even his big machines, painted under the influence of Roman Mannerism, are redeemed by brilliant effects of lighting, flames, night scenes, or sunshine streaming into a dark place.

73

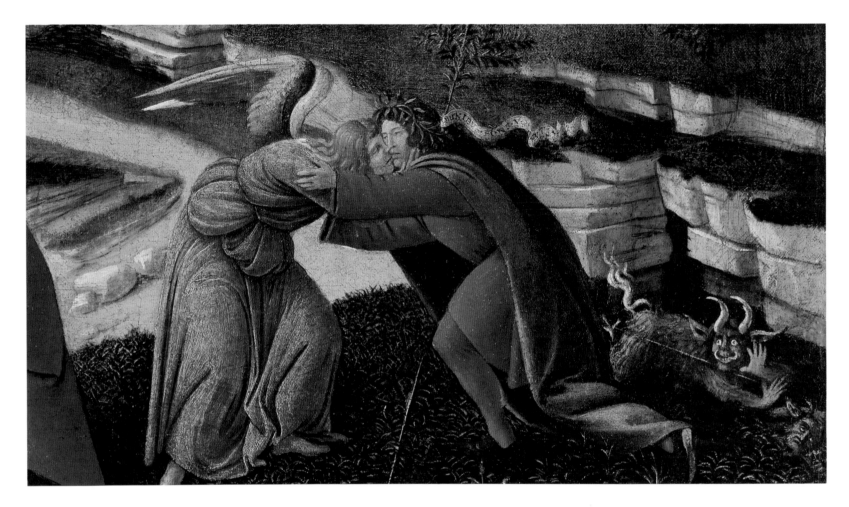

From the MYSTIC NATIVITY *by Botticelli,
painted about 1500.*

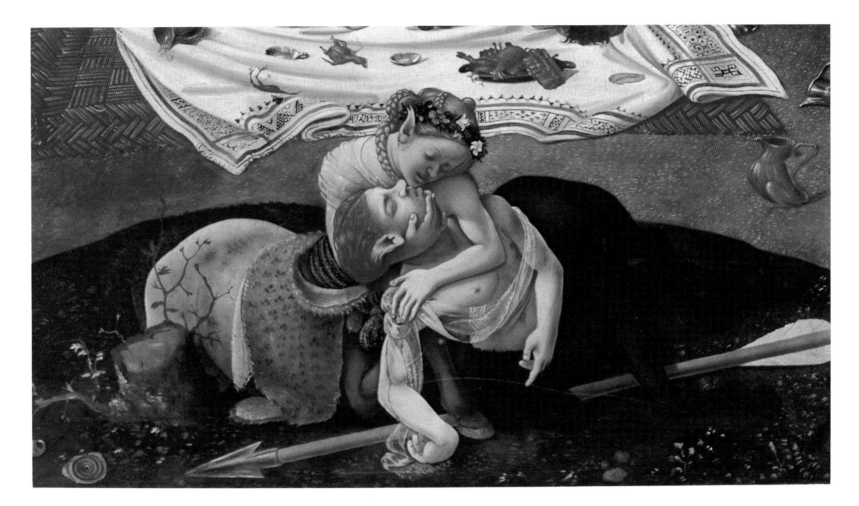

Centaurs from **THE FIGHT BETWEEN THE LAPITHS AND THE CENTAURS** *by Piero di Cosimo, painted about 1500.*

Perhaps sacred and profane love. Botticelli has expressed the disembodied joy of certain passages in Dante's *Paradiso*, but as a rule the sacred love of the mystics is far more sensuous. Language, even the language of Oriental eroticism, can be interpreted symbolically, but shapes declare themselves without equivocation. So in this phase of Puritanism, Botticelli, the most delicate master of sensuous beauty, must hide the human body in voluminous, unrevealing draperies. Piero di Cosimo's centaurs are extraordinarily touching. To their human tenderness is added a dumb animal pathos of which he is the unique interpreter. This group is so absorbing as poetry that we do not at once realise the skill with which Piero di Cosimo has solved an unusual problem: how to make a good composition out of two recumbent centaurs. Their inverted heads and the elaborate arabesque of their arms show a mastery of design which he never surpassed.

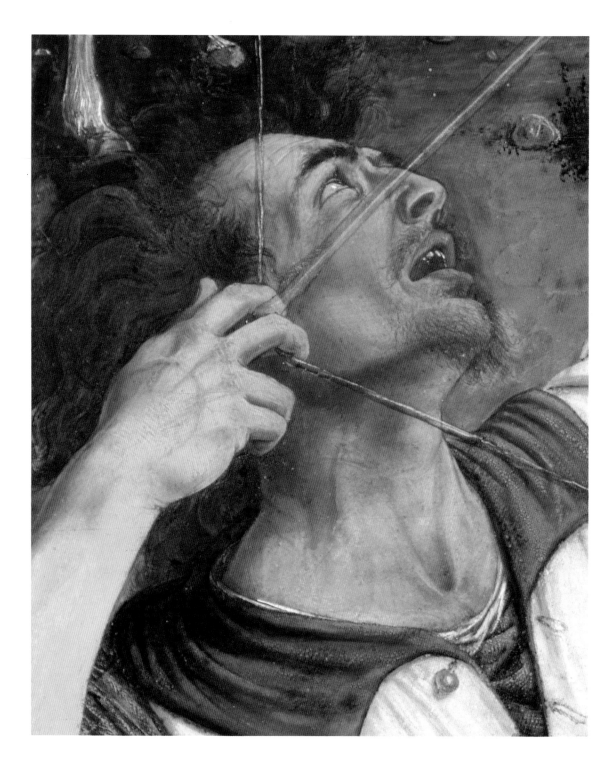

An archer from
THE MARTYRDOM OF
SAINT SEBASTIAN, *by*
Antonio and Piero del
Pollaiuolo, painted about 1475.

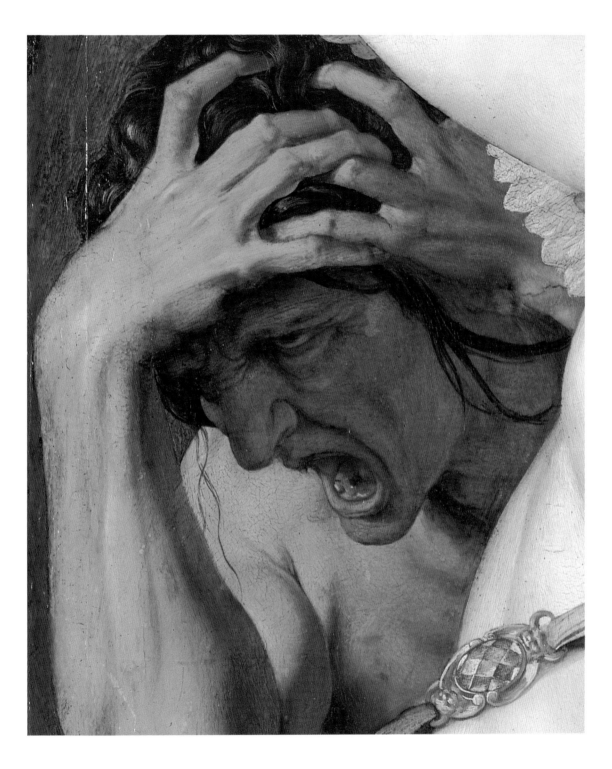

Envy from AN ALLEGORY WITH VENUS AND CUPID *by Bronzino, painted about the 1540s.*

This magnificent opening shows the continuity of the Florentine tradition. The two pictures are separated by almost seventy years, yet both painters are interested in the same forms, and depict them with the same balance of line and modelling. Only in Envy's expression do we feel a shade of exaggeration, deriving no doubt from Leonardo's *Battle of Anghiari* (Palazzo Vecchio, Florence), which reminds us that Bronzino lived in the age of Mannerism.

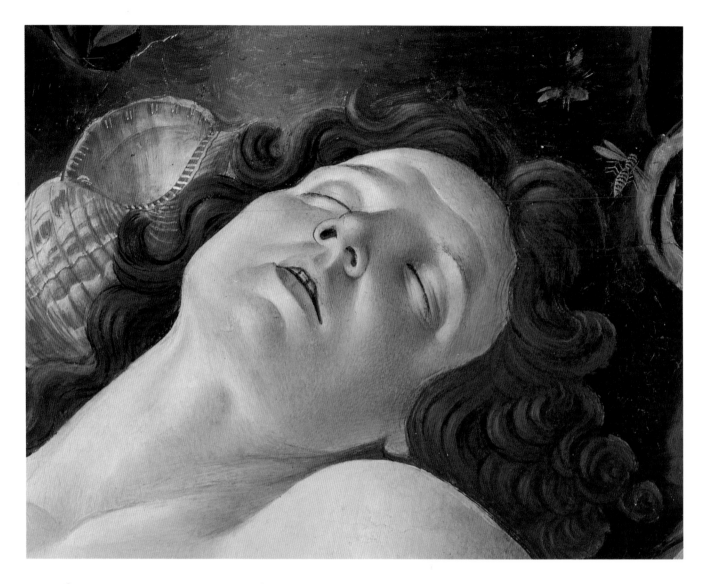

Mars from VENUS AND MARS *by Botticelli,
painted about 1480.*

Even in Botticelli's day a fine foreshortening was
considered a proof of ability. But he sets about his
problems in a spirit very different from that of Mantegna
or of those German artists whom Dürer has shown us
drawing the foreshortened figure through a squared
projector. His aim is not accuracy but expressiveness. A
drawing master might make some corrections in Mars'
head, but these would certainly destroy the movement of
the planes and the feeling of utter relaxation which is its
chief beauty.

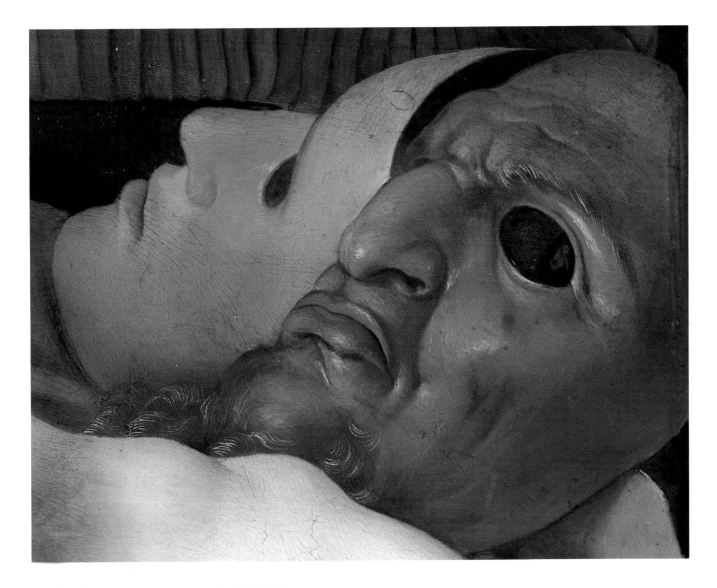

Masks from AN ALLEGORY WITH
VENUS AND CUPID *by Bronzino, painted
about the 1540s.*

Classical masks play an important part in the late
Renaissance, since they were one of the few ways in
which the grotesque, the unreal, the gargoyle element
in art could be introduced with propriety. Even
Michelangelo put them into the Medici Chapel in
Florence, and Bronzino may have had in mind the noble
mask which lies beside Michelangelo's figure of Night
when he designed the masks in this detail. It is the sort of
homage which the Florentine academics would have
been glad to pay to their divinity. Actually Bronzino's
masks have a literary significance, for they lie at the feet
of Fraud and Folly, and are part of the allegory of
passion, which is the real subject of the picture.

The Virgin from THE
VIRGIN AND CHILD,
*ascribed to Verrocchio, painted
about 1480.*

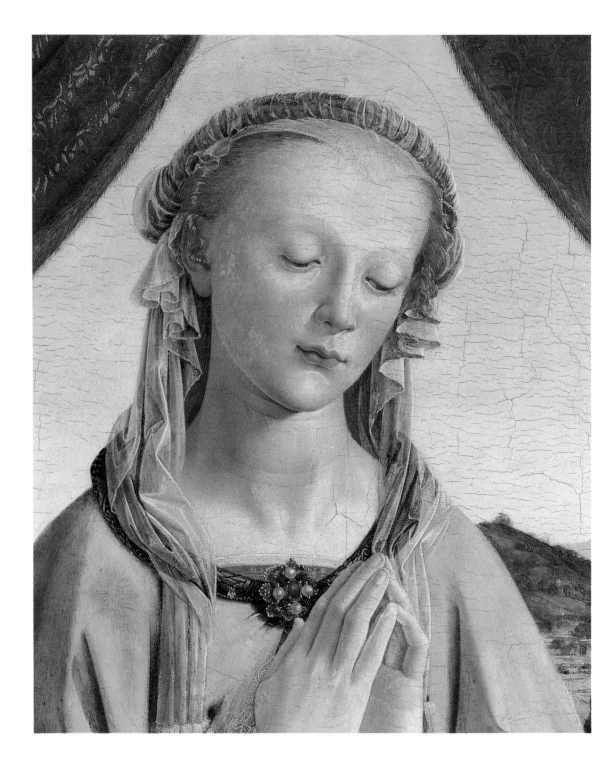

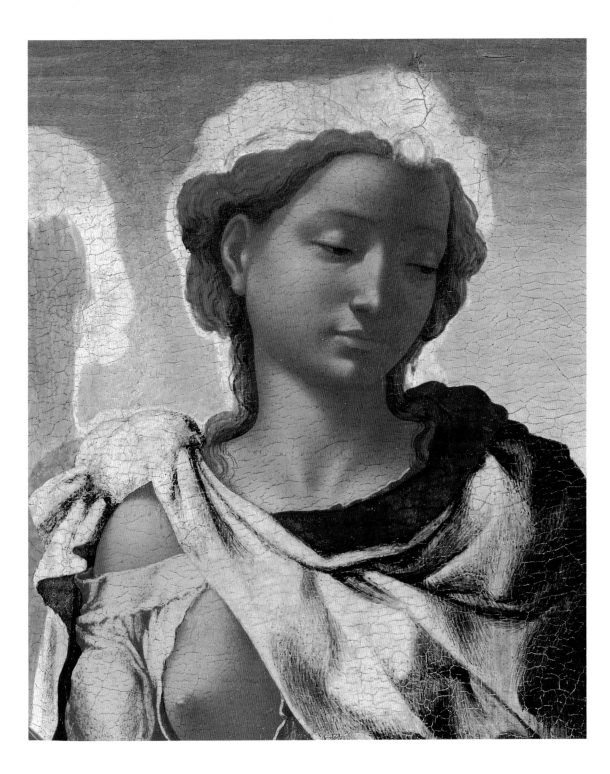

The Virgin from THE
MADONNA AND CHILD,
*ascribed to Michelangelo,
painted about 1500.*

The authenticity of the Michelangelo
has often been questioned, and some
critical opinion is still against it, but
a comparison of these two details
speaks strongly in its favour. In
general movement they are
remarkably alike. They clearly
belong to the same tradition, and no
one seeing them together could
maintain, as has been done, that the
Michelangelo is by a late sixteenth-
century Mannerist. On the other
hand they are strikingly different,
and only a great artist could make
Verrocchio look so feeble and
conventional. In spite of a certain
youthful clumsiness, Michelangelo's
Madonna has true, unmistakable
force and nobility, perceptible in
every touch. This detail shows clearly
the strokes of the brush like strokes
of the chisel on a block of marble,
which will remind every amateur of
Michelangelo's early pen drawings.

The Virgin from THE
ANSIDEI MADONNA
by Raphael, painted in 1505.

Raphael sails very near the wind.
Cold, insipid, complacent, academic
– all these words are on the tips of
our tongues, as they are when we
read certain passages of Racine, and
with as little justification. What saves
him? First of all his supreme skill, of
which this head shows one aspect,
the economy with which he could
achieve an unsurpassed degree of
plastic fullness. And then there is
in Raphael, as in Racine and Mozart,
an inner rhythm which is perceptible
in every touch, and allows great
precision without loss of grace or
vitality. From another hand the
drawing of the Virgin's eyes would
have been schematic; and the parallel
shading round her cheek would have
been as lifeless as a line engraving.
With Raphael all the weapons of
academic technique become as
sensitive and springy as a rapier.

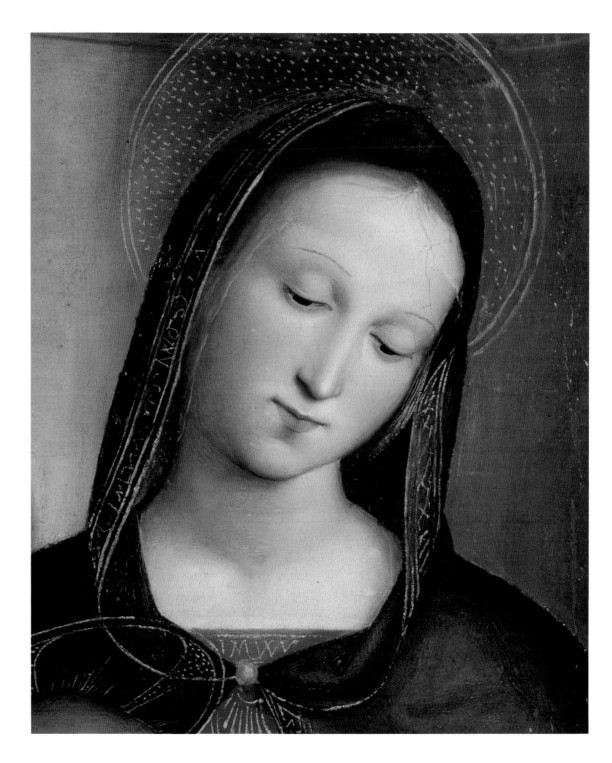

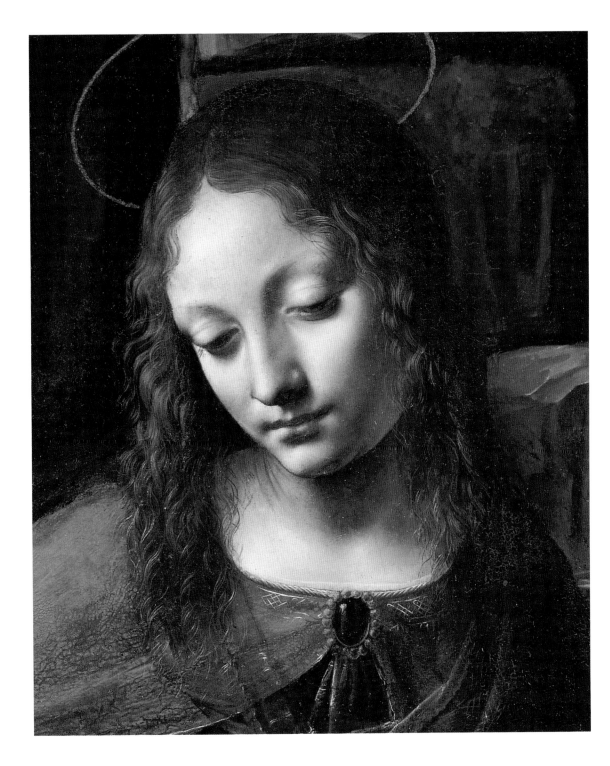

The Virgin from THE VIRGIN OF THE ROCKS *by Leonardo da Vinci, painted about 1508.*

There is no longer any doubt that the National Gallery's *Virgin of the Rocks* is a second version of the subject undertaken by Leonardo some twenty years after the picture in the Louvre. Exactly why he was commissioned to paint this later version is unknown but a most probable reason is that the original had been sent to France at the order of Louis XII, and Leonardo was asked to make a replica for the Confraternity of the Immaculate Conception to which the original had belonged. It is uncertain how much of this replica he executed with his own hand, and this head of the Virgin is the most difficult part of the problem. It is too heavy and lifeless for Leonardo and the actual type is un-Leonardesque; yet it seems to be painted in exactly the same technique as the angel's head in the same picture (Plate 97); and that is so perfect that surely Leonardo must have had a hand in it. Both show curious marks of palm and thumb (they are visible in this detail on the bridge of the Virgin's nose) made when the paint was wet, and no doubt covered by glazes long since removed. This perhaps is a clue to the problem. A pupil did the main work of drawing and modelling, and before his paint was dry Leonardo put in the finishing touches. Most of these have been removed from the Virgin's face but remain in the angel's, where perhaps they were always more numerous.[7]

[7] As a result of the cleaning of the altarpiece in 1949 the differences between the heads are perhaps less apparent.

83

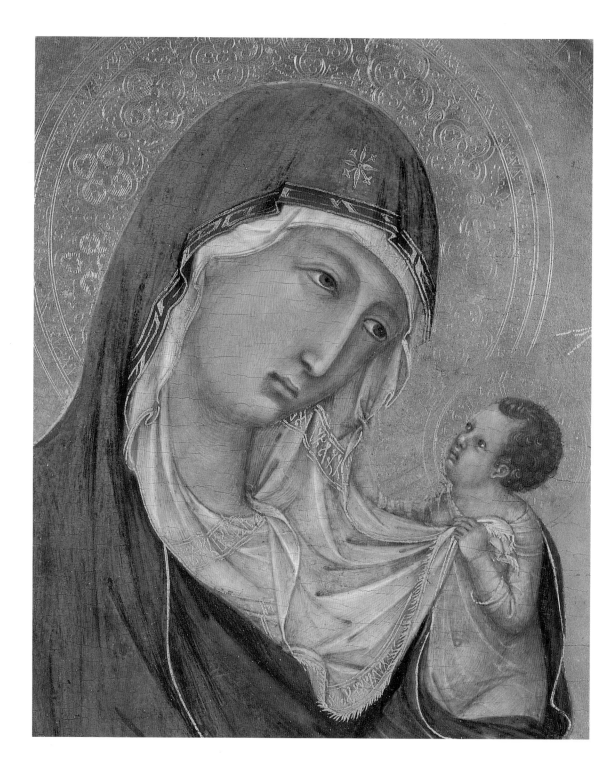

From THE VIRGIN AND
CHILD WITH SAINTS *by*
Duccio, painted about 1315.

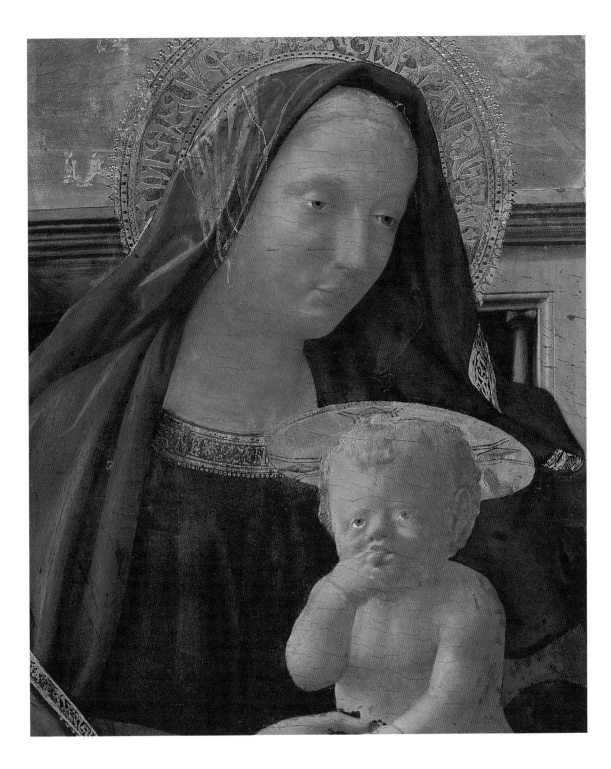

Between these two Madonnas there lies the emergence of that new scheme of human values which was one of the great conquests of Renaissance art. The Duccio is not lacking in tenderness, but this only makes itself felt to one whose eye is accustomed to his style. He speaks to us in an ancient, elegant, formal language, perfected two hundred years earlier in Constantinople, after centuries of attrition. Even Masaccio's Madonna shows some memory of this style in the large rhythms of the composition; but essentially she is a new creation, born of a direct and serious contemplation of nature. Never before and seldom again has a painter had the courage to make his Madonna a plain, natural woman who does not derive her authority from conventional beauty, but from the moral grandeur latent in her expression. Compared with her, the Madonnas of Giotto and Michelangelo are too imperious, those of Botticelli and Fra Filippo too pathetic: only Bellini, in the Brera *Pietà* (Milan), has created a similar type of common humanity raised to the divine.

85

The Angel Gabriel from
THE ANNUNCIATION
by Fra Filippo Lippi, painted about 1448.

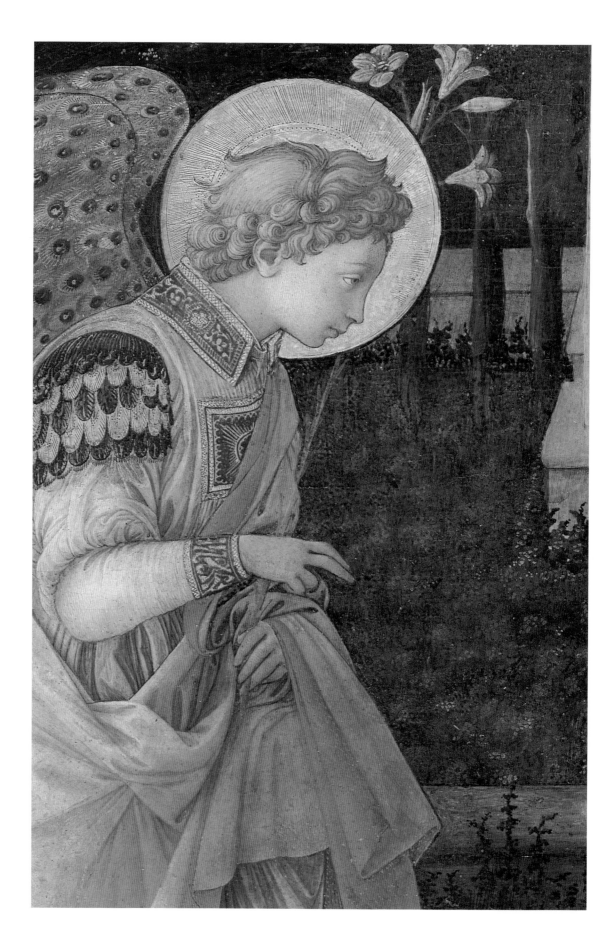

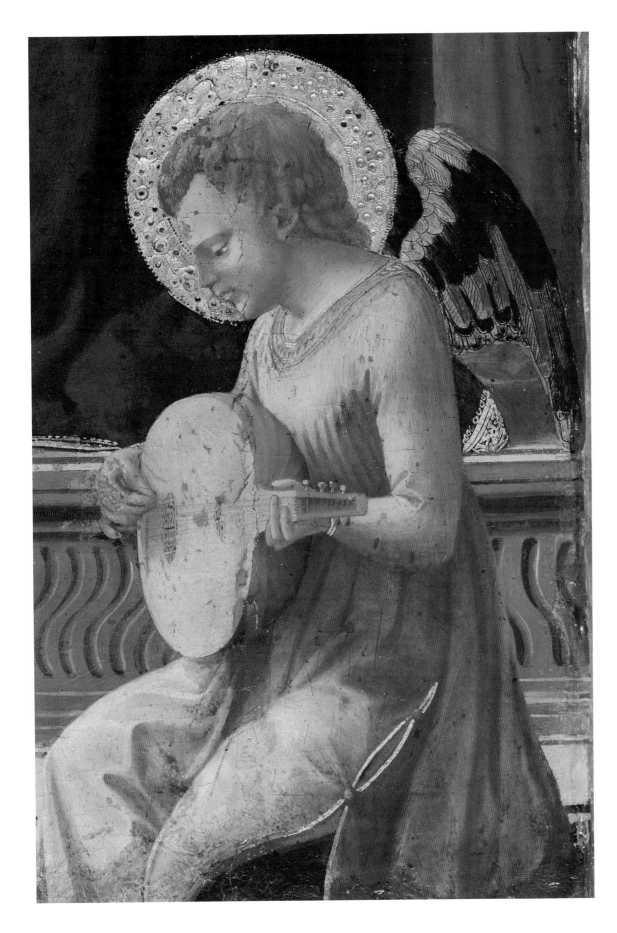

An angel from THE VIRGIN AND CHILD *by Masaccio, painted in 1426.*

Fra Filippo's angel expresses that same Florentine feeling for graceful movement which we find in Lorenzo Monaco and Botticelli (Plates 34 and 35). It stands in time midway between them. We see that this linear tradition in Florentine art was unbroken, and expressed a more continuous need than the tradition of scientific naturalism, of which Masaccio's angel is a small but sturdy representative. Up to a point it is true to say that this linear style was popular and aristocratic, whereas the solid, scientific style of Masaccio was only appreciated by the humanists and intellectual bourgeoisie. Yet Fra Filippo was a favourite painter of the Medici, and *The Annunciation* was almost certainly painted for a member of the Medici family.

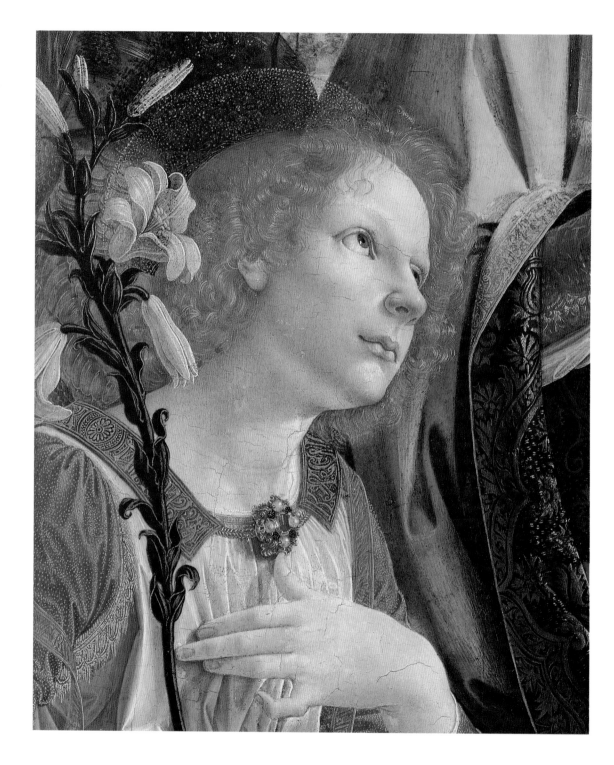

An angel from THE VIRGIN AND CHILD, *ascribed to Verrocchio, painted about 1480.*

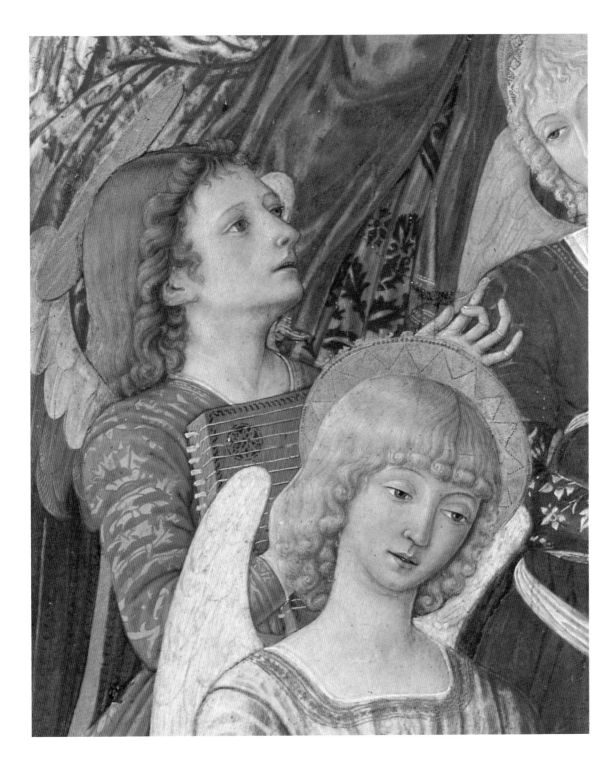

Angels from
THE ASSUMPTION OF THE VIRGIN *by Matteo di Giovanni, painted about 1474.*

As a comparison between Sienese and Florentine painting this is unfair on Florence, because Matteo's picture is one of the masterpieces of its school, which Verrocchio's is not. In fact, it is little more than a piece of high-class craftsmanship, the kind of picture you bought at a goldsmith's shop, where you might also buy the original of the pretty brooch worn by the angel. However, it serves to show the chief aims of Florentine drawing: to make the human form look solid. The Sienese thought of drawing as involving balance of line and pattern. In the detail from Matteo di Giovanni, wings, draperies and the musical instruments are an accompaniment to the angels' heads, whereas in the Verrocchio they are only a distraction.

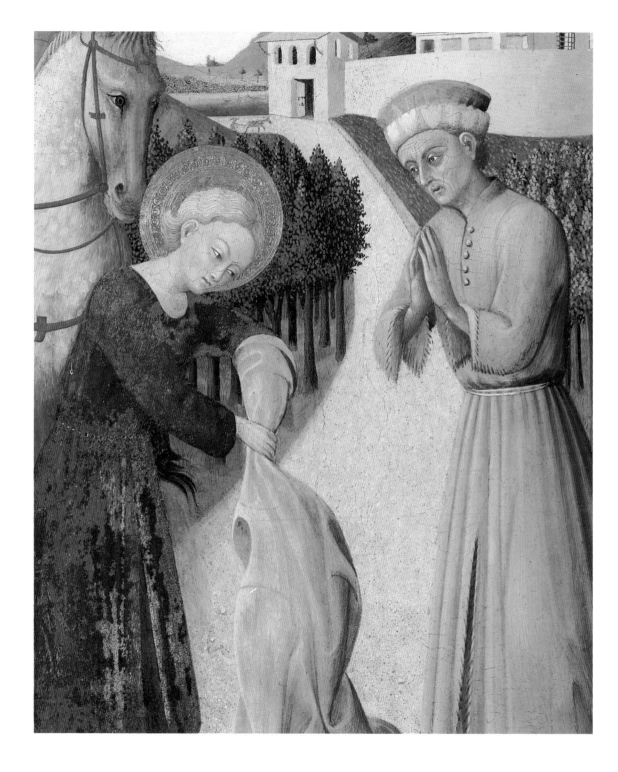

Saint Francis gives his cloak to the poor gentleman from THE WISH OF THE YOUNG SAINT FRANCIS TO BECOME A SOLDIER *by Sassetta, panel from an altarpiece commissioned in 1437, completed in 1444.*

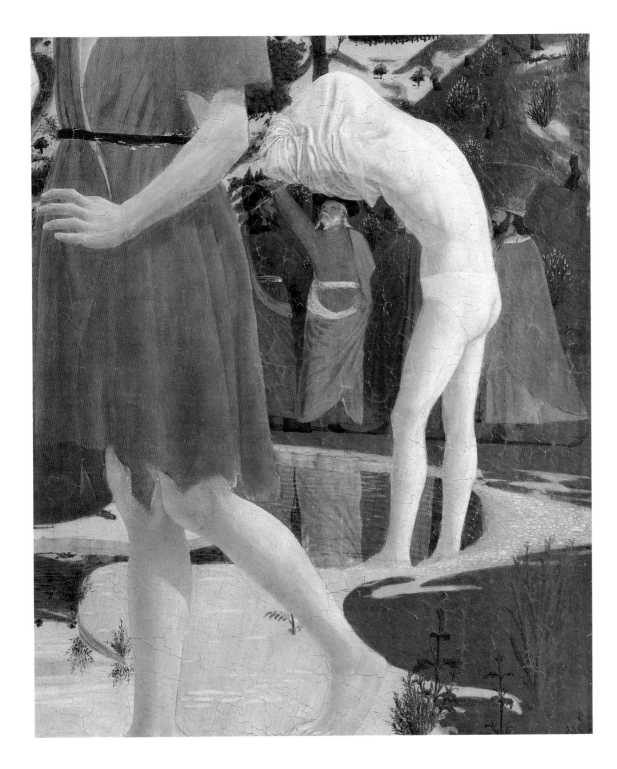

From THE BAPTISM OF CHRIST *by Piero della Francesca, painted about 1450.*

Most of the comparisons in this book bridge wide intervals of time and space; this one is the reverse. Piero's *Baptism* and Sassetta's *Scenes from the Life of Saint Francis of Assisi* were painted for the small town of Borgo san Sepolcro in the same period, and both artists were influenced by the same masters, Masolino and, in particular, Domenico Veneziano. From the latter they derived a pale, luminous atmosphere which Sassetta soon abandoned, but which Piero made one of the bases of his style.

Though temporarily united by this joy in silvery tone, they are essentially different. Sassetta is still Gothic. His road shoots up at an impossible angle, and all his forms harmonise with this sharp Gothic movement. The curve of Piero's river bank is slow and classical. All his forms have the measured deliberation of antique architecture, and the man taking off his shirt, which Vasari praised for its naturalism, might have come from the Acropolis.

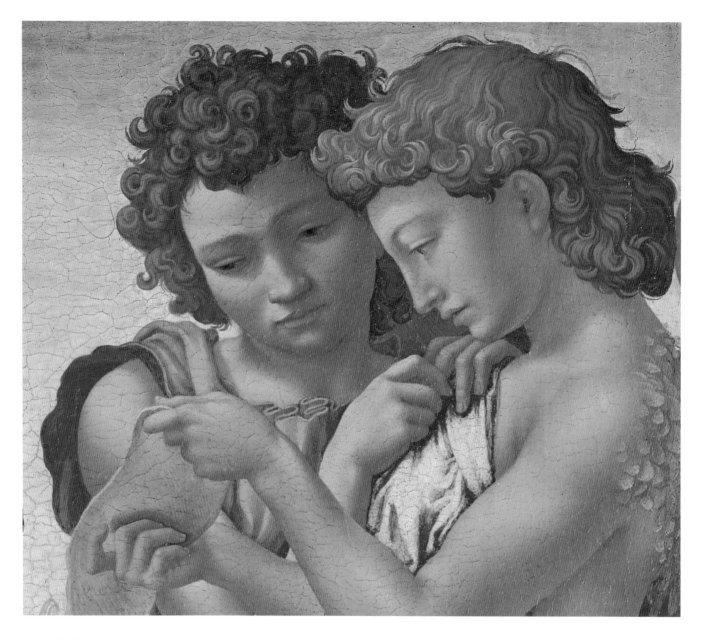

Angels from THE MADONNA AND
CHILD, *ascribed to Michelangelo, painted
about 1500.*

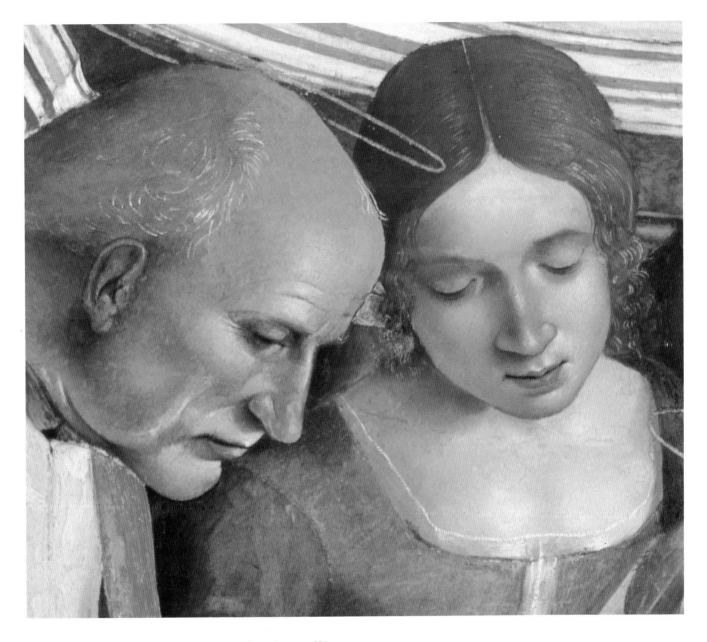

From THE CIRCUMCISION *by Signorelli, painted about 1491.*

Signorelli was one of the most consistently serious of all great artists. He never allowed himself any of the humour or fantasy which we find in almost all the painters of the Renaissance, and even his *Triumph of Pan* in the Berlin Museum is conceived in terms of great solemnity. This seriousness, no less than his interest in the nude, is his link with Michelangelo. If, as I believe, the National Gallery's *Madonna and Child* is by the young Michelangelo, it probably dates from around 1500; yet the affinity with Signorelli is already obvious. In a note to Plates 80 and 81 I have given some reasons why the old attribution of the National Gallery picture to Michelangelo cannot be dismissed without consideration. In this detail it is worth noticing how closely these two youths resemble, in character and morphology, the figures carved by Michelangelo for the Ark of Saint Dominic, Bologna, in 1494; and in particular the Saint Proculus which, I would suggest, is a self portrait of Michelangelo himself as a young man.

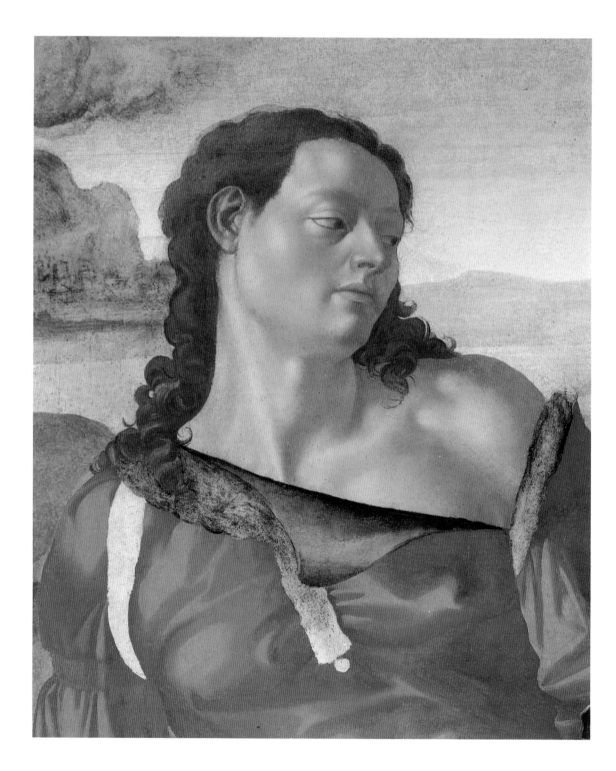

94

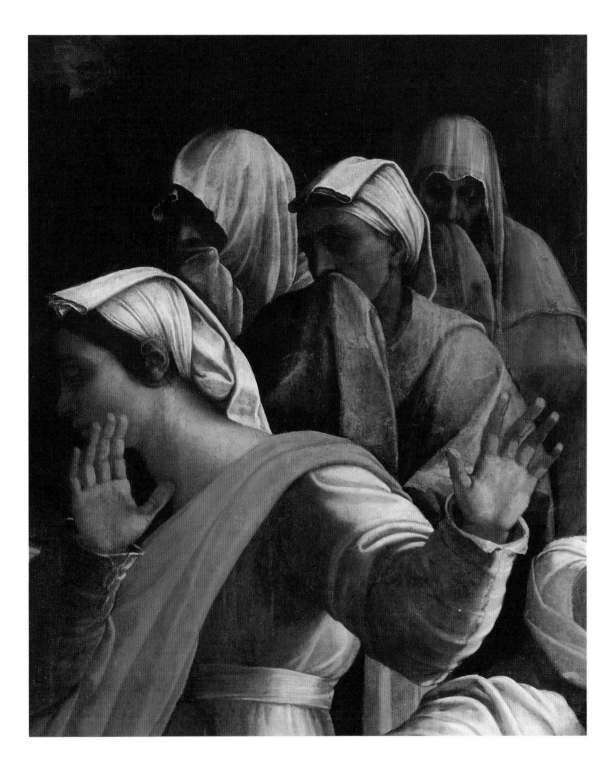

The Grand Manner, that painful obsession of European art, is a personal endowment. It is like a noble gesture which cannot be imitated without becoming empty and theatrical. In no one has this endowment been so strong as in Michelangelo who, from his earliest youth, could not make a mark which was devoid of grandeur; with the result that for centuries ambitious artists were led to their ruin. Sebastiano del Piombo was the first of the long line which culminated in Benjamin Robert Haydon: not that the Grand Manner drove Sebastiano to suicide, only it left him so exhausted that after receiving a pension from the Pope he never painted again and lived solely for gossip and the pleasures of the table. His efforts to assume the Grand Manner were remarkably successful, for he was close to the source of that dangerous illumination. It was easier for him to glow with reflected glory when Michelangelo stood beside him, and, as we are told, even provided drawings for *The Raising of Lazarus*. We can believe that the group in this detail, which in sentiment and to some extent in form anticipates that unforgettable group of women in the Cappella Paolina fresco of *Saint Peter's Crucifixion* in the Vatican, derives from a sketch by Michelangelo who often foreshadowed in his studies motifs which were only brought to mature expression many years later.

95

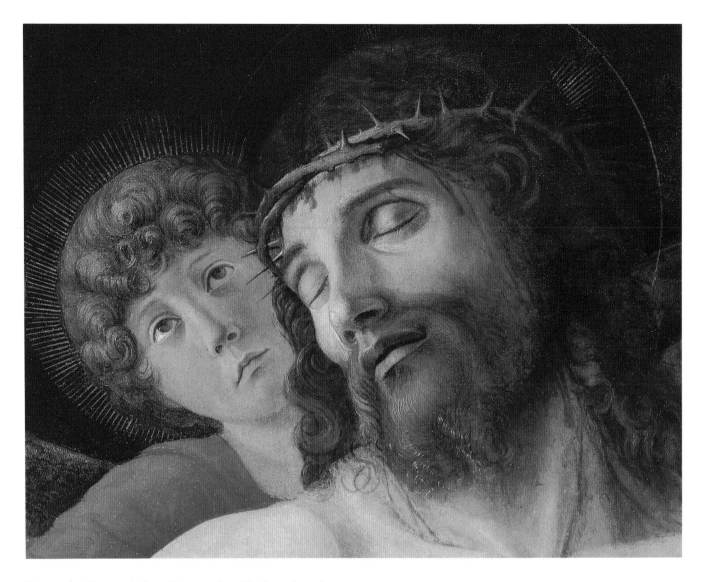

From the PIETA *by Giovanni Bellini, painted about 1470.*

Often in his treatment of solemn themes Bellini indulges in conscious archaism, and this is particularly true of the period round about 1475 when his Madonnas show the influence of Byzantine painting. The Mond *Pietà* belongs to these years, and in this detail the angel's head is deliberately archaic. This simplified oval has the added value that it does not distract from the complex plastic sequences of the head of Christ.

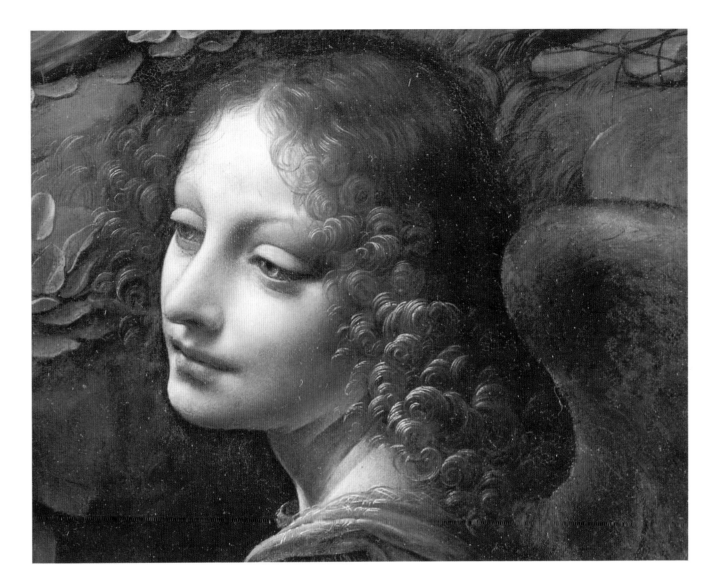

The angel from THE VIRGIN OF THE ROCKS *by Leonardo da Vinci, painted about 1508.*

This is the one part of the National Gallery's *Virgin of the Rocks* where the evidence of Leonardo's hand seems undeniable (see note to Plate 83), not only in the full, simple modelling, but in the drawing of the hair. The curls round the shoulder have exactly the same movement as Leonardo's drawings of swirling water. Beautiful as it is, this angel lacks the enchantment of the lighter, more Gothic angel in the Paris version. It embodies the result of Leonardo's later researches in which ideal beauty and classic regularity of chiaroscuro were combined, with a certain loss in freshness, but with an expressive power which almost hypnotised his contemporaries.

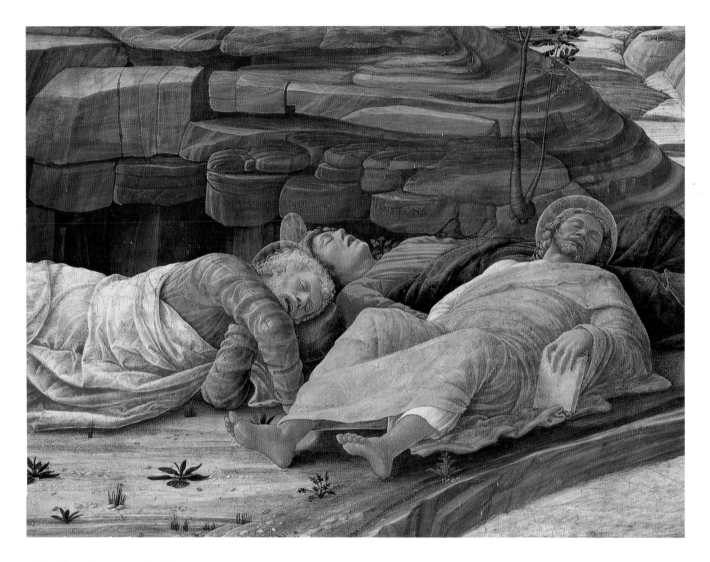

The sleeping Apostles from THE AGONY IN
THE GARDEN *by Mantegna, painted in
the 1460s.*

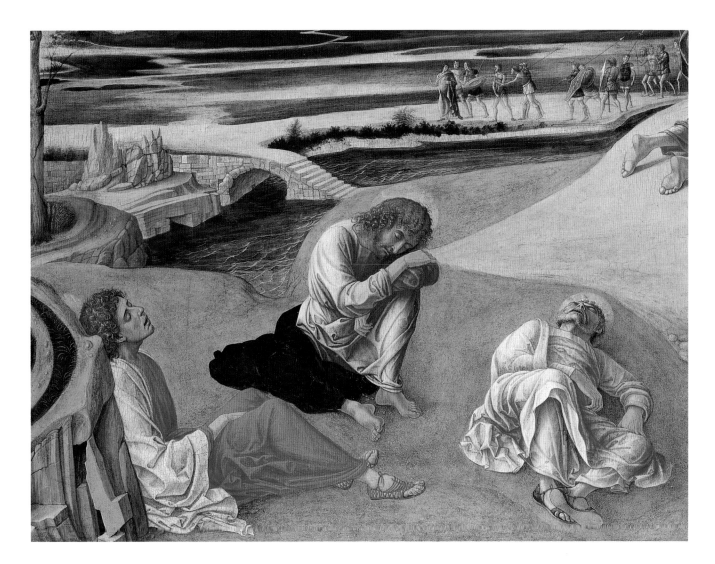

The sleeping Apostles from THE AGONY IN THE GARDEN *by Giovanni Bellini, painted about 1465.*

It is a piece of wonderful good fortune that two great pictures of the same subject, probably painted at the same time by men who were intimately related to one another, should hang together in the National Gallery; and in comparing them generations of amateurs must have learnt one of their first and finest lessons in the appreciation of Italian art. The comparison provided by these two details of the sleeping Apostles is unfair on Bellini. His drawing looks cramped and immature beside the grasp and grandeur of Mantegna. We can understand why he always spoke of his brother-in-law with such deep respect and, even in old age, wrote to Isabella d'Este that he did not feel worthy to paint in a room already decorated by Mantegna. (However, this may only have been an excuse to avoid working for a troublesome patron.) Yet even in this detail we are aware of Bellini's unrivalled feeling for light, and his Apostles have a human pathos which makes Mantegna seem a little too intellectual. A wise critic in 1460, comparing the work of these two youngish artists, might have admitted Mantegna's greater mastery but seen in Bellini a passionate love of nature which promised a fuller development. And in fact Mantegna remained set in his classic mould, while Bellini revealed, till past his eightieth year, new depths of poetry and humanity.

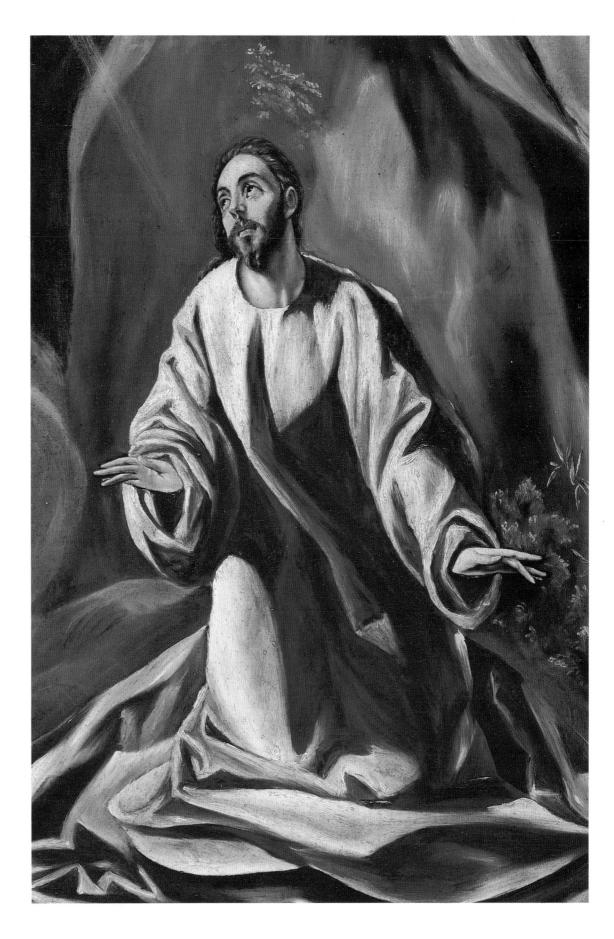

Christist from **THE AGONY IN THE GARDEN,** *painted in El Greco's studio, about 1600.*

Index of Paintings

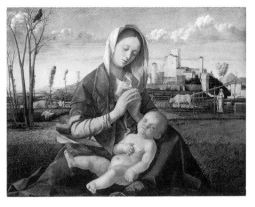

Giovanni BELLINI active about 1459; died 1516
Plate 23 *The Madonna of the Meadow* (599)
Canvas transferred from wood,
painted area 67.3 × 86.4 cm (26½ × 34 in)

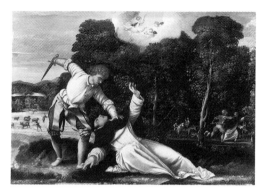

Ascribed to BERNARDINO da Asola recorded 1526
Plate 62 *The Death of Saint Peter Martyr* (41)
Canvas, 101.5 × 144.8 cm (40¼ × 57 in)

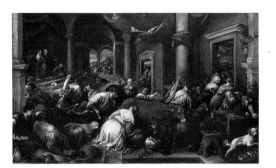

Jacopo BASSANO active about 1535; died 1592
Plate 20 *The Purification of the Temple* (228)
Canvas, 158.7 × 265 cm (62½ × 104½ in)

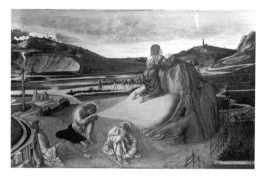

Giovanni BELLINI active about 1459; died 1516
Plates 41, 99 *The Agony in the Garden* (726)
Wood, painted area 81.3 × 127 cm (32 × 50 in)

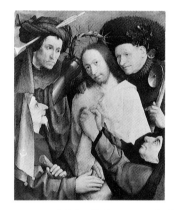

Hieronymus BOSCH living 1474; died 1516
Plate 14 *Christ Mocked*
('The Crowning with Thorns') (4744)
Wood (oak),
painted area 73.5 × 59.1 cm (29 × 23¼ in)

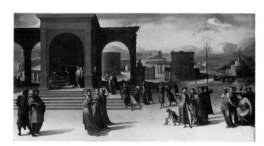

Domenico BECCAFUMI 1486(?)–1551
Plate 73 *An Unidentified Scene* (1430)
Wood, 74 × 137.8 cm (29⅛ × 54¼ in)

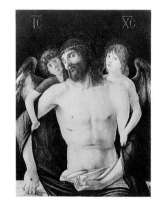

Giovanni BELLINI active about 1459; died 1516
Plate 96 *Pietà* (3912)
Wood, painted area 94.6 × 71.8 cm (37¼ × 28¼ in)

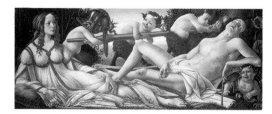

Sandro BOTTICELLI about 1445–1510
Plates 4, 78 *Venus and Mars* (915)
Wood, painted area (sight size)
69.2 × 173.4 cm (27¼ × 68¼ in)

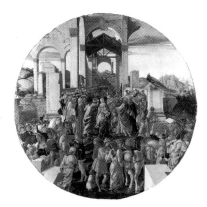

Sandro BOTTICELLI about 1445–1510
Plate 72 *The Adoration of the Kings* (1033)
Wood, tondo,
painted area diameter 130.8 cm (51½ in)

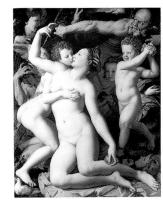

BRONZINO 1503–1572
Plates 77, 79 *An Allegory with Venus and Cupid* (651)
Wood, 146.1 × 116.2 cm (57½ × 45¾ in)

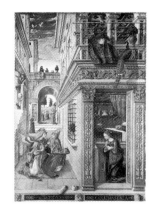

Carlo CRIVELLI active 1457 to 1493
Plate 10 *Altarpiece: The Annunciation,
with Saint Emidius* (739)
Wood, transferred to canvas,
painted area 207 × 146.7 cm (81½ × 57¾ in)

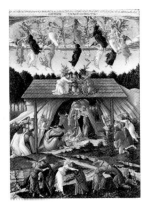

Sandro BOTTICELLI about 1445–1510
Plates 34, 38, 74 *'Mystic Nativity'* (1034)
Canvas, 108.6 × 74.9 cm (42¾ × 29½ in)

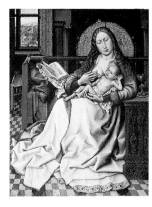

Robert CAMPIN 1378/9–1444
Plate 11 *The Virgin and Child
before a Fire-screen* (2609)
Wood (oak),
painted area 63.5 × 49.5 cm (25 × 19¼ in)

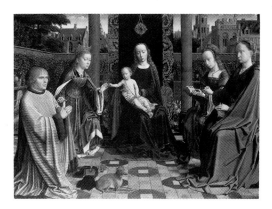

Gerard DAVID active 1484; died 1523
Plate 8 *The Virgin and Child
with Saints and Donor* (1432)
Wood (oak),
painted area 106 × 144.1 cm (41¾ × 56¾ in)

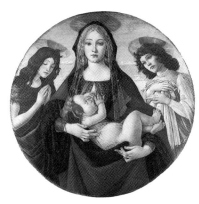

Studio of BOTTICELLI
Plate 37 *The Virgin and Child with
Saint John and an Angel* (275)
Wood, tondo
painted area 84.4 cm (33¼ in)

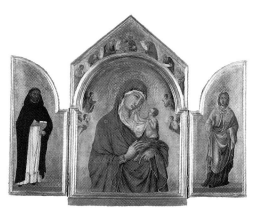

CORREGGIO active 1514; died 1534
Plates 56, 60 *Mercury instructing Cupid
before Venus ('The School of Love')* (10)
Canvas, 155.6 × 91.4 cm (61¼ × 36 in)

DUCCIO active 1278; died 1319
Plate 84 *Triptych: The Virgin
and Child with Saints* (566)
Wood, pointed top, total size of central panel
including the framing, the tympanum and the base
61.3 × 39 cm (24⅛ × 15⅜ in)

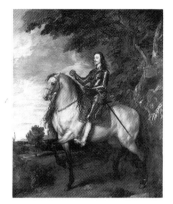

Anthony van DYCK 1599–1641
Plate 49 *Equestrian Portrait of Charles I* (1172)
Canvas, approximately 367 × 292.1 cm (144½ × 115 in)

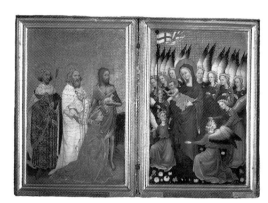

FRENCH School (?), about 1395 or later
Plate 30 *Richard II presented to the Virgin
and Child by his Patron Saints
('The Wilton Diptych')* (4451)
Wood (oak),
each panel painted area 47.5 × 29.2 cm (18 × 11½ in)

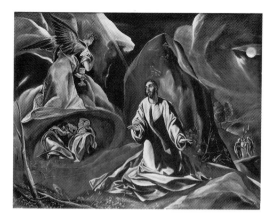

Studio of EL GRECO 1541–1614
Plates 39, 100 *The Agony in the
Garden of Gethsemane* (3476)
Canvas, 102 × 131 cm (40 × 51½ in)

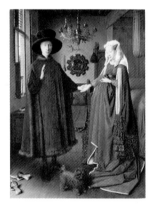

Jan van EYCK active 1422; died 1441
Plates 2, 5 *The Marriage of Giovanni
Arnolfini and Giovanna Cenami ('The
Arnolfini Marriage')* (186) Wood (oak),
painted area 81.8 × 59.7 cm (32¼ × 23½ in)

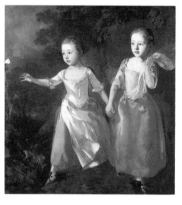

Thomas GAINSBOROUGH 1727–1788
Plate 25 *The Painter's Daughters
chasing a Butterfly* (1811)
Canvas, 113.7 × 104.8 cm (44¾ × 41¼ in)

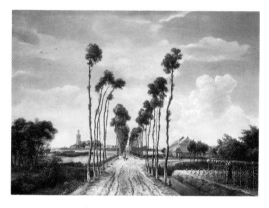

Meyndert HOBBEMA 1638–1709
Plate 43 *The Avenue, Middelharnis* (830)
Canvas, 103.5 × 141 cm (40¾ × 55½ in)

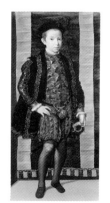

FLORENTINE School (?), 16th Century
Plate 24 *Portrait of a Boy* (649)
Wood, 128.9 × 61 cm (50¾ × 24 in)

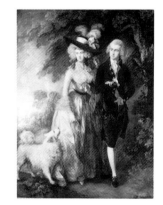

Thomas GAINSBOROUGH 1727–1788
Plate 46 *The Morning Walk* (6209)
Canvas, 236.2 × 179.1 cm (93 × 70½ in)

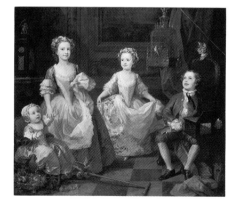

William HOGARTH 1697–1764
Plate 54 *The Graham Children* (4756)
160.5 × 181 cm (63½ × 71¼ in)

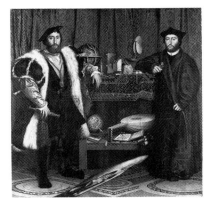

Hans HOLBEIN the Younger 1497/8–1543
Plates 44, 50 *Jean de Dinteville and
Georges de Selve ('The Ambassadors')* (1314)
Wood (oak),
painted area 207 × 209.5 cm (81½ × 82½ in)

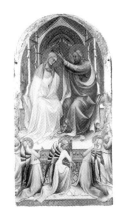

LEONARDO da Vinci 1452–1519
Plates 83, 97 *The Virgin of the Rocks*
(Central Panel from an Altarpiece) (1093)
Wood, rounded top,
painted area 189.5 × 120 cm (74⅝ × 47¼ in)

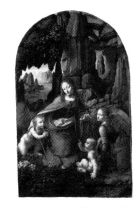

LORENZO Monaco before 1372–1422 or later
Plate 35 *The Coronation of the Virgin*
(Central Part of an Altarpiece) (1897)
Wood, pointed top,
painted area 217.2 × 115.6 cm (85½ × 45½ in)

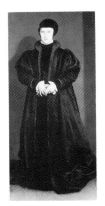

Hans HOLBEIN the Younger 1497/8–1543
Plates 51, 59 *Christina of Denmark,
Duchess of Milan* (2475)
Wood (oak),
painted area 179.1 × 82.6 cm (70½ × 32½ in)

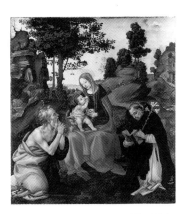

Filippino LIPPI 1457(?)–1504
Plate 65 *Altarpiece: The Virgin and Child
with Saints Jerome and Dominic* (293)
Wood, main panel painted area approximately
203.2 × 186.1 cm (80 × 73½ in)

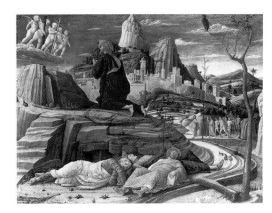

Andrea MANTEGNA about 1430/1–1506
Plate 98 *The Agony in the Garden* (1417)
Wood, painted area 62.9 × 80 cm (24¾ × 31½ in)

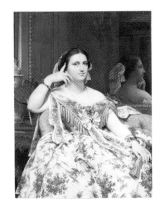

Jean-Auguste-Dominique INGRES 1780–1867
Plate 52 *Madame Moitessier* (4821)
Canvas, 120 × 92.1 cm (47¼ × 36¼ in)

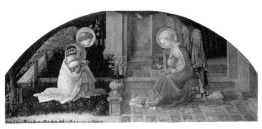

Fra Filippo LIPPI 1406(?)–1469
Plate 86 *The Annunciation* (666)
Wood, rounded top, 68.6 × 152.4 cm (27 × 60 in)

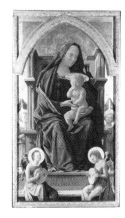

MASACCIO 1401–1427/9
Plates 85, 87 *The Virgin and Child*
(Central Part of an Altarpiece) (3046)
Wood, pointed top,
painted area 135.3 × 73 cm (53¼ × 28¾ in)

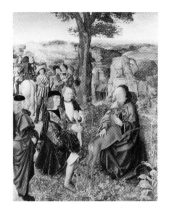

MASTER OF SAINT GILES active about 1500
Plate 6 *Saint Giles and the Hind* (1419)
Wood (oak),
painted area 61.6 × 46.4 cm (24¼ × 18¼ in)

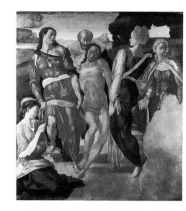

MICHELANGELO 1475–1564
Plate 94 *The Entombment* (790)
Wood, 161.7 × 149.9 cm (63⅔ × 59 in); unfinished

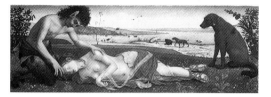

PIERO di Cosimo about 1462– after 1515
Plates 12, 55 *A Mythological Subject* (698)
Wood, painted area 65.4 × 184.2 cm (23¾ × 72¼ in)

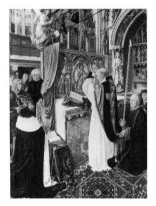

MASTER OF SAINT GILES active about 1500
Plate 9 *The Mass of Saint Giles* (4681)
Wood (oak),
painted area 61.6 × 45.7 cm (24¼ × 18 in)

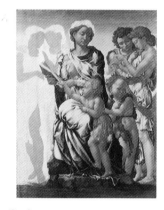

Ascribed to MICHELANGELO 1475–1564
Plates 81, 92 *The Madonna and Child with Saint
John and Angels ('The Manchester Madonna')* (809)
Tempera (mainly) on wood,
105.4 × 76.8 cm (41½ × 30¼ in); unfinished

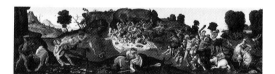

PIERO di Cosimo about 1462– after 1515
Plate 75 *The Fight between the Lapiths
and the Centaurs* (4890)
Wood, painted area 71 × 260 cm (28 × 102½ in)

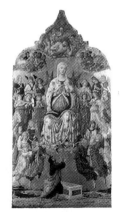

MATTEO di Giovanni active 1452; died 1495
Plates 33, 36, 89 *The Assumption of the Virgin
(Central Panel from an Altarpiece)* (1155)
Wood, irregular top,
331.5 × 174 cm (130½ × 68½ in)

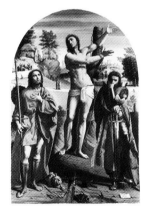

L'ORTOLANO born before 1487; still active 1524
Plate 15 *Altarpiece: Saints Sebastian,
Roch and Demetrius* (669)
Wood, transferred to canvas, arched top,
230.4 × 154.9 cm (90¾ × 61 in)

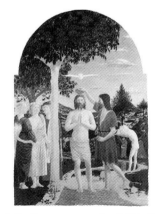

PIERO della Francesca active 1439; died 1492
Plates 32, 40, 91 *The Baptism of Christ
(Part ? of an Altarpiece)* (665)
Wood, rounded top,
painted area, 167 × 116 cm (66 × 45¾ in)

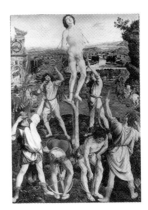

Antonio del POLLAIUOLO
about 1432–1498 and
Piero del POLLAIUOLO born about 1441;
died before 1496
Plates 7, 26, 76 *Altarpiece: The Martyrdom*
of Saint Sebastian (292)
Wood, 291.5 × 202.6 cm (114¾ × 79¾ in)

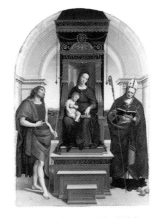

RAPHAEL 1483–1520
Plates 3, 82 *Altarpiece: The Madonna and Child*
with Saint John the Baptist and Saint Nicholas
of Bari ('The Ansidei Madonna') (1171)
Wood, arched top,
painted area 209.6 × 148.6 cm (82½ × 58½ in)

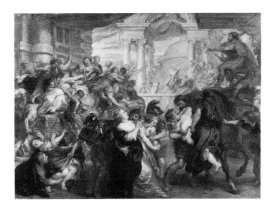

Peter Paul RUBENS 1577–1640
Plate 19 *The Rape of the Sabine Women* (38)
Wood, 169.9 × 236.2 cm (66⅞ × 93 in)

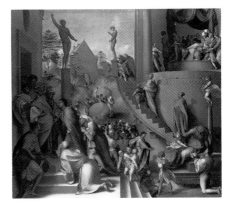

PONTORMO 1494–1557
Plates 29, 68 *Joseph with Jacob in Egypt* (1131)
Wood, painted area 96.5 × 109.5 cm (38 × 43⅛ in)

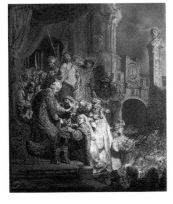

REMBRANDT 1606–1669
Plate 21 *Christ presented to the People*
('Ecce Homo') (1400)
Grisaille on paper, stuck on canvas,
54.5 × 44.5 cm (21⁷⁄₁₆ × 17½ in)

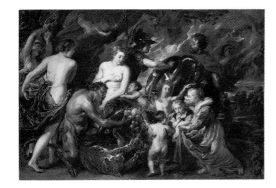

Peter Paul RUBENS 1577–1640
Plate 13 *Minerva protects Pax from Mars*
('Peace and War') (46)
Canvas,
approximately 203.5 × 298 cm (80⅛ × 117⁵⁄₁₆ in)

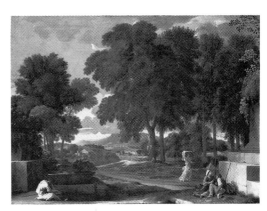

Attributed to Nicolas POUSSIN 1594(?)–1665
Plate 28 *Landscape with a Man washing*
his Feet at a Fountain (40)
Canvas 74.3 × 100.3 cm (29¼ × 39½ in)

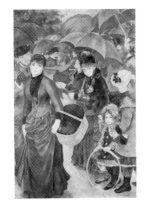

Pierre-Auguste RENOIR 1841–1919
Plate 47 *The Umbrellas (Les Parapluies)* (3268)
Canvas, 180.3 × 114.9 cm (71 × 45¼ in)

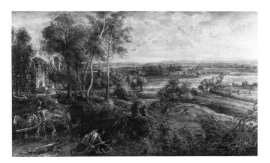

Peter Paul RUBENS 1577–1640
Plate 27 *An Autumn Landscape with a View*
of Het Steen in the Early Morning (66)
Wood (oak),
approximately 131.2 × 229.2 cm (51⅝ × 90¼ in)

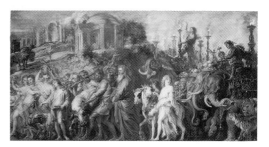

Peter Paul RUBENS 1577–1640
Plate 16 *A Roman Triumph* (278)
Canvas, 86.8 × 163.9 cm (34⅛ × 64½ in)

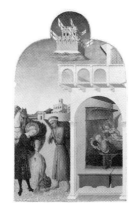

SASSETTA 1392(?)–1450
Plates 31, 90 *The Wish of the Young
Saint Francis to become a Soldier*
(Panel from an Altarpiece) (4757)
Wood, trefoiled top,
painted area 87 × 52.4 cm (34¼ × 20⅝ in)

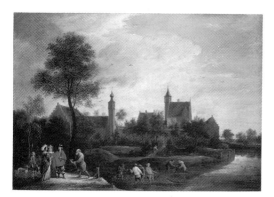

David TENIERS the Younger 1610–1690
Plate 42 *A View of Het Sterckshof
near Antwerp* (817)
Canvas, 82 × 118 cm (32¼ × 46⁹⁄₁₆ in)

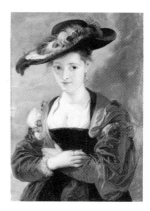

Peter Paul RUBENS 1577–1640
Plates 53, 58 *Portrait of Susanna Lunden
('Le Chapeau de Paille')* (852)
Wood (oak),
approximately 79 × 54 cm (3¹⁄₁₆ × 21¼ in)

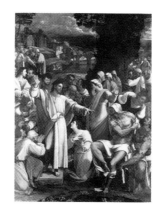

SEBASTIANO del Piombo about 1485–1547
Plate 95 *The Raising of Lazarus* (1)
Wood, transferred to canvas and remounted on board,
approximately 381 × 289.6 cm (150 × 114 in)

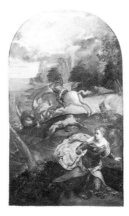

Jacopo TINTORETTO 1518–1594
Plates 63, 66 *Saint George and the Dragon* (16)
Canvas, arched top, 157.5 × 100.3 cm (62 × 39½ in)

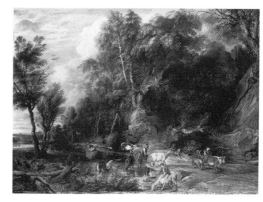

Peter Paul RUBENS 1577–1640
Plate 22 *Peasants with Cattle by a Stream in
a Woody Landscape ('The Watering Place')* (4815)
Black chalk and oil on wood (oak),
approximately 98.7 × 135 cm (38⅞ × 52¹⁵⁄₁₆ in)

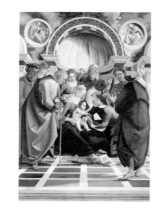

Luca SIGNORELLI 1441(?)–1523
Plate 93 *Altarpiece: The Circumcision* (1128)
Wood, painted area 258.5 × 180 cm (101¾ × 71 in)

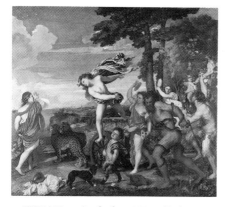

TITIAN active before 1511; died 1576
Plates 64, 67 *Bacchus and Ariadne* (35)
Canvas, 175.2 × 190.5 cm (69 × 75 in)

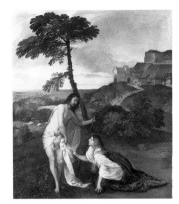

TITIAN active before 1511; died 1576
Plate 70 *Christ appearing to the Magdalen*
('Noli me Tangere') (270)
Canvas, 108.6 × 90.8 cm (42¾ × 35¾ in)

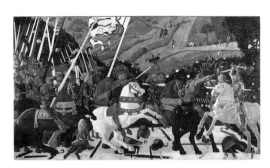

Paolo UCCELLO about 1397–1475
Plates 1, 17 *Niccolò Mauruzi da Tolentino at*
the Battle of San Romano (From a Series) (583)
Wood, painted area 181.6 × 320 cm (71½ × 126 in)

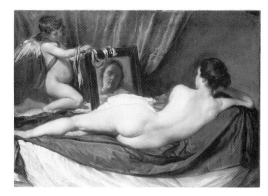

Diego VELAZQUEZ 1599–1660
Plate 57 *The Toilet of Venus*
('The Rokeby Venus') (2057)
Canvas,
approximately 122.5 × 177 cm (48¼ × 69¾ in)

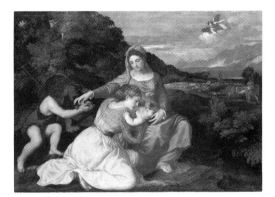

TITIAN active before 1511; died 1576
Plate 71 *Madonna and Child with Saints John*
the Baptist and Catherine of Alexandria (635)
Canvas, 100.6 × 142.2 cm (39⅝ × 56 in)

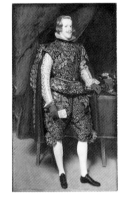

Diego VELAZQUEZ 1599–1660
Plate 48 *Philip IV of Spain*
in Brown and Silver (1129)
Canvas, approximately 195 × 110 cm (76⅞ × 43¼ in)

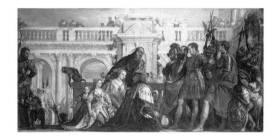

Paolo VERONESE 1528(?)–1588
Plates 18, 61 *The Family of Darius*
before Alexander (294)
Canvas, 236.2 × 474.9 cm (93 × 187 in)

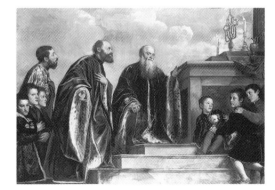

TITIAN active before 1511; died 1576
Plate 69 *The Vendramin Family* (4452)
Canvas, 205.7 × 301 cm (81 × 118½ in)

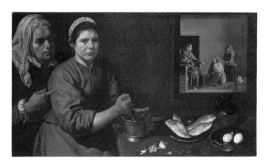

Diego VELAZQUEZ 1599–1660
Plate 45 *Kitchen Scene with Christ in the*
House of Martha and Mary (1375)
Canvas, 60 × 103.5 cm (23⅝ × 40¾ in)

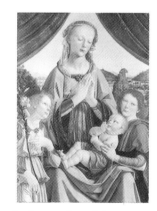

Ascribed to Andrea del VERROCCHIO
about 1435–1488
Plates 80, 88 *The Virgin and Child*
with Two Angels (296)
Wood, painted area 96.5 × 70.5 cm (38 × 27¾ in)